GIRLFRIENDS GUIDE TO MONEY

Me...? Write for a financial book? who ever would have thought?!? love you. Molly p.96

GIRLFRIENDS GUIDE TO
MONEY

Your Math-Free, Guilt-Free Guide
to Financial Health

Lucinda Atwood, Ann Leckie
and Marina Glass

iUniverse, Inc.
Bloomington

Girlfriends Guide to Money
Your Math-Free, Guilt-Free Guide to Financial Health

iUniverse books may be ordered through booksellers or by contacting:

iUniverse
1663 Liberty Drive
Bloomington, IN 47403
www.iuniverse.com
1-800-Authors (1-800-288-4677)

Because of the dynamic nature of the Internet, any web addresses or links contained in this book may have changed since publication and may no longer be valid. The views expressed in this work are solely those of the authors and do not necessarily reflect the views of the publisher, and the publisher hereby disclaims any responsibility for them.

ISBN: 978-1-4620-5607-1 (sc)
ISBN: 978-1-4620-5609-5 (hc)
ISBN: 978-1-4620-5608-8 (e)

Library of Congress Control Number: 2011917154

iUniverse rev. date: 09/26/2011

Contents

Section One

Section Two

Endnotes

Do You Want to Improve your Relationship with Money?

"I'm sorry, it's been declined. Do you have another card?" The cashier hands back your debit card. Trying to look unconcerned, you pull out a credit card. Hopefully that one will go through; two declines would be embarrassing.

Oh well, it's only a week until payday, you can live on credit that long. But still, it's only the 25th; last month you made it to the 28th before running out of cash. It seems that each month, the month gets longer and the cash gets shorter. One of these days you're going to do something about that. And start a savings account. Imagine going on a real vacation …

Which reminds you to buy a lottery ticket, or as you call it, the retirement fund.

Do you experience money as a source of sadness, jealousy, anger, resentment, confusion or worry? Many of us do. We want to be responsible, but feel out of control with our money. We work so hard to earn it, but there never seems to be enough. We know what we should be doing, but nothing seems to work, at least not for long. We are not weak or stupid, but somehow money seems unmanageable.

Spending is no fun either. Paying the bills is depressing; so much of our money goes for expenses. We feel guilty spending on ourselves, so we overspend in other areas. Or we overspend on ourselves, but still feel unsatisfied.

These negative emotions diminish the quality of our lives.

This Book will Help You Change your Relationship with Money

Ask yourself these questions:

1. Do you have credit card debt?
2. Do you worry about *which* bills to pay this month, knowing that you can't afford to pay all of them?
3. Did you and your partner argue about money this month?
4. Do you feel anxious about money?
5. In the past month, did you save less than you think you should have?
6. Do you ever feel jealous when friends go on a trip or to an expensive restaurant, or buy new shoes?
7. Are you thinking about working longer hours or getting a second job in order to pay the bills? But worrying about missing out even more with your kids or partner?
8. Do you feel that you should be doing more for family or groups you believe in such as community, religion or charities, but can't due to lack of time and money?
9. Do you worry about your financial future?
10. Do you worry about your children's relationship with money? Do you get upset when they ask you to buy things? Do they constantly beg you to buy things?

11. In the past month, did you buy something only because it was cheap?
12. In the past month, did you deny yourself an experience or item that you really wanted, only because of the cost?

If you answered yes to any of these questions, you have the potential to improve the quality of your life by improving your relationship with money.

Your relationship with money has nothing to do with the amount of money that you have. Read that sentence again: **Your relationship with money has nothing to do with the amount of money that you have.**

Your sense of abundance and financial health is affected by your thoughts about money, the way you interact with it, and how you perceive the role money plays in your life. When you spend and save according to your values and goals, you will feel sufficient and abundant. You will get what you want.

How you think and feel about money greatly affects your sense of abundance and your ability to have enough. Changing your relationship with money *can* change your life.

This book was written to give you an option; to offer you a new way of thinking about abundance, your values and your money. You *can* create a positive and joyous — yes joyous — relationship with money.

This book will help you to:

• Develop a healthy relationship with money.
• Manage your money confidently.

- Spend and save in alignment with your goals and values.
- Make saving and managing your money an easy and positive aspect of your life.
- Develop a network of professionals and experts who can help you manage your money at specific times in your life.

This Book will Help Others

When you improve your relationship with money, you will influence your friends, family and co-workers. You will model healthy attitudes and open the door to understanding that *rich is a state of mind.*

By living your values, your life will improve and you will touch the lives of others. You will free up money to donate to charities and good causes.

And, yes, you can still have nice shoes!

Listen up, Girlfriend …

We wrote this book as a "girlfriends" guide to money. Think of us as your girlfriends, walking beside you, supporting you. We are the girlfriends you turn to when your relationship goes bad, who listen with open hearts and then tell it like it is.

We like you. We believe in you. We believe that you — as you are — are sufficient. You have everything you need to have a healthy relationship with money; all you need is the insight to evolve your thinking.

When you believe in yourself the way we believe in you, your relationship with money will change. You will have enough. You will find yourself spending and saving in alignment with your values.

What this Book is Not

This book is not a lecture — we are not here to tell you what you have done wrong or how to live. We will not encourage you to get rid of all your possessions or to stop shopping.

This book is not about numbers and equations. It contains no math and none of those gut-wrenching, headache-inducing exercises that make most of us feel guilty and incapable.

Who Are We?

Lucinda Atwood, Ann Leckie and Marina Glass

We are three friends who saw women giving their power away through lack of knowledge, awareness and support. We have experienced the move from lack to abundance. We know the joy of spending *and* saving in alignment with our values. Our goal is to help you develop a great relationship with money so that you too can live happily and fully.

The three of us have backgrounds in finance, human resources, community development, writing, design and fine art. Between us we have five children, two husbands, three cars, one dog, two cats and a gerbil. We practice taekwondo, triathlon, soccer, yoga, abundance and living the best lives we can.

Last fall we began power walking together. We were each at a place of change in our lives, and our brisk morning walk became a great way to ground ourselves and act as sounding boards for each other's various projects and problems. It didn't take us long to recognize that money was a common thread. A lot of issues with kids, husbands, mortgages, divorce, employment, childcare, school and quality of life include some aspect of financial management.

Ann had just helped a client company with a large merger and was surprised that none of the employees had come to the HR (Human Resources) department for help or support. Ann, who lives and breathes HR, was stunned to realize that many people aren't even aware of the services available, much less how to access them.

Marina says, "My life has included enough financial disasters that Ann's newfound awareness resonated with me. I'd been one of those people who didn't know where to get help or how to ask. When something major happens, you don't know what you need to know, how to get help, or even that help is available. Self-education is time consuming and can be frustrating. Experience taught me to get help — as much as possible, as early as possible — and to arm myself with knowledge and surround myself with good people."

Lucinda was re-establishing her life as a single mother, and realizing how disconnected she had allowed herself to become from her finances, always trusting and deferring to her husband's judgment. "Like any stereotypical writer or artist, I hated talking about money because I never thought it was very important. But Ann kept talking about it! Finally I realized that I needed and wanted to face my financial reality. Life was different for me now; I could no longer stick my head in the sand and make finances someone else's responsibility."

Money plays a huge part in our lives and our perceptions of happiness. Money management is rarely taught in school, but it's one of the most important aspects of living in our society. We don't think money should be worshipped or vilified, but we all need to understand what to expect from money, and how to manage it in alignment with our goals and values.

By living the values espoused in this book, we can afford to support our communities. We donate 20% of the profits from this book to Covenant House, an organization making a difference in our community.

How (and When) to Use this Book

This book can set the tone for your future interactions with money and how you earn, spend and save. We recommend that you read it before you read other money books, before you get into numbers and equations, and that you keep it handy as a reference for each new chapter in your life. Review it at each new stage of your life: when you go to school, look for employment, buy a house, start a family, and make business decisions.

In Section One, we guide you to financial health by exploring your values and developing financial goals and action plans.

An important part of financial health is a support network that will help you through hard times; no matter what you have to go through, you don't have to do it alone. A good network incudes experts and professionals, so in Section Two we introduce you to some of our "Expert Girlfriends". Each expert shares information about what to do and how to manage specific times and events that can affect your financial health.

We hope you find the ideas and exercises as useful as we have. We had such a great time writing this book that we are continuing the conversation. Follow us on Twitter at @moneygirlfriend or on our Facebook page *Girlfriends Guide to Money*, and come visit us at GirlfriendsGuidetoMoney.com. We have great conversations, articles, worksheets and creative activities. You can learn more about us and introduce yourself. We'd love to hear your story!

1. Understanding your Relationship with Money

Many of us in North America have been blessed with abundance, yet often feel deprived. We see people in advertisements and the media who appear to be perfect, happy and young. Images abound of beautiful people in glorious clothes living wonderful lives. Each image is carefully crafted to exploit our secret yearning to be desired and desirable. Each ad says if you were included, powerful and rich, you would have this already. And if you had this, you would be included, powerful and rich!

We want to be those people. We want to trade our boring little lives in for their glamour and acclaim. We think that we would be happy if we had what they have, so we participate in an endless cycle of buy, upgrade, then buy some more. We constantly consume, trying to make our lives somehow better or more meaningful.

Why Doesn't Buying Things Make Us Feel Better?

If having the latest fashion, toy or technology is supposed to make us happy, why are so many of us feeling worse?

The answer is simple. It's not necessarily the things that we purchase that are the problem; it's *why we purchase* that has gone awry. There are several reasons that so many of us have negative relationships with money:

1. We mistake the adrenaline rush of shopping for true joy and contentment.
2. We mistakenly believe that if only we had more things we would be happy.
3. We do not understand that we are enough, and feel that having more or better things will make us sufficient or acceptable.
4. We see flaws in ourselves and believe that they can be fixed with things or money.

Entire businesses are built around these beliefs. Skin care, beauty products, designer fashion, house wares and expensive cars — we can't buy this stuff fast enough. We are always looking for more and better to fill that hole within us.

But our solution of consuming to fill the hole doesn't work. It's a pattern of spending that does not reflect our inner values and does not bring happiness. Even if we do buy something we want and think we need, something even more fancy and "necessary" comes along. The hole within us never fills. We are as emotionally empty as before.

We Need to Heal our Relationship with Money

No one is suggesting that we stop spending money. We do need to buy things — food, clothing, shelter and transportation are important; so is rewarding ourselves. But mindless consumerism and driving ourselves into debt and stress will not make us happy. *Things* will not make us different or transform our lives.

Ann remembers being in Disneyland last year. "It was late and people were heading home. Everyone looked tired; kids were cranky and whiney. I sat down on a bench to rest, and a couple sat beside me with their crying two year old. The woman turned to her man and said, 'This is why I want a divorce!' Over their heads was a sign: *The Happiest Place on Earth.* The irony didn't escape me. They went on holiday and spent tons of money but they were no happier. You can't buy happiness."

We work hard to earn money to feed, clothe and shelter our families. We want — and deserve — rewards and fun. We need — and deserve — to be relaxed with money; to enjoy earning, spending and saving it. We also deserve the peace that comes from knowing that we are managing our money well according to our own values.

Sufficiency

We need to develop a sense of sufficiency. That what we have is enough. For those of us who have the basics but never feel satisfied and rack up thousands a year in mindless debt, we say STOP. Let's look at what is really going on, and understand that we already have enough. We are enough.

But I Love Pretty Shoes!

Sufficiency doesn't mean that we Girlfriends don't like pretty things. We certainly do. We still see a gorgeous pair of shoes and say, "I want them!"

The difference is that we don't define ourselves around those shoes. We don't think that we will be happier if we buy them or somehow diminished if we don't.

We know the secret of having proper expectations of the things that we buy. We know that those shoes can't transform our lives. We don't expect them to help us get, keep or dump that boyfriend. We don't expect those shoes to do anything other than what they are designed to do — look pretty and help support us as we move forward.

We know that true happiness comes from living in alignment with our values. And while we enjoy the fun of a good purchase, we don't confuse it with happiness.

We live with a sense of abundance because we know what we want and how to get it. We spend and save in alignment with our values.

We know that we can admire and even desire an item and walk away without buying it — *and survive*. (It's true!) We know that if one sweater makes us happy, ten will not necessarily make us ten times happier. We know that buying a mirrored side table will not undo this morning's fight with Sweetie-pie.

Positive Attitudes

We know that you can have a positive relationship with money; one that is healthy, balanced, and joyous. Yes joyous! A positive relationship with money is not built around the power of more. It rests on these positive attitudes:

- Acceptance of trade-offs
- Openness
- Control
- Lack of jealousy and judgment
- Optimism

Acceptance of Trade-offs

A positive relationship with money acknowledges that there will always be trade-offs. For example, going to school means forgoing earnings. For some of us that is a good trade-off. For others, it's not worth it.

Sometimes it feels that you are forever trading things off. You might say, "I went into debt to pay for school. Then I got married and saved up for a house; now we have kids … when will this be done? When do the trade-offs end?"

Of course, the answer is never. Money is a finite resource, which means that there will always be trade-offs. Even the richest of the rich can't have everything.

Marina accepted trade-offs after she bought a very large and beautiful home. "We loved the house and could afford it when we bought it. With children, economic downturns and a family crisis we were in a different situation. We decided to keep our home, which meant making drastic changes to our lifestyle. Looking back, I'm happy with the choices and compromises we made at that time."

You are in control of your relationship with money. If you don't like the trade-offs you make, you can change them. Years later,

Marina reviewed the trade-offs she makes to live in her house. She realized that she was no longer willing to put in all the time and energy necessary to maintain it. She decided to sell and find a home that needs less upkeep.

Openness

Openness acknowledges that money, just like every aspect of your life, calls for trade-offs. It is being honest about how that feels — both the good and the bad. You don't have to tell anyone what you earn, how much you spent on something, or where you bought it. However, openness makes for great girlfriend conversation and a great attitude towards money.

Openness goes like this: "I saw a wonderful outfit for sale and wanted to buy it. Then I realized that if I made that choice I would have to forgo going out to lunch for a week. That wasn't a trade-off I wanted to make, so I didn't get the outfit. For a moment it hurt that I couldn't have both, but now, sitting at lunch with you, I know that I made the right choice. I love hanging out with you!"

Control

Being in control of your money means spending and saving according to your values. Control creates balance and empowerment in you and your finances.

Self-control is one of the most important aspects of success in finance, business and life. Self-control means being able to manage yourself so that you can achieve your goals. It's being able

to remember what is important to you in the face of perfect sweaters and red sports cars; to want and walk away no less happy.

We're not saying to punish yourself for buying that sparkly bracelet back in '02, or to never reward yourself. Being in control of your spending creates a positive relationship with money, but taken to extremes it can be bad for your emotional and financial health.

It is has been proven that binge dieting — starving yourself for a period of time — does not work. Similarly, binge saving does not work. When you deny yourself even a little reward or luxury, you hold yourself like a tightly wound spring. The tension will eventually explode into a crazed buying spree. As a response to the famine of penny-pinching, you will probably spend more than you would have normally.

Both over-control and lack of control create chaos in your financial life. Aim for balance.

Lack of Jealousy and Judgment

Jealousy — that evil green-eyed monster. Jealousy drives destructive competitive behaviors and has destroyed lives and relationships. A lack of jealousy is freeing. It allows you to be truly happy for your friend when she buys a new car or gorgeous shoes.

We see wonderful dresses at the Oscars and think "Wow, they're beautiful!" Are we jealous? No! We can't imagine needing dresses like that. Ann says that while she admires the gowns, "I don't want one because I have no place to wear it. The dressiest places I frequent are offices and if I wore a ball gown to work ... well, it would be odd to say the least. To be able to wear those kinds of clothes I'd have to attend formal events, which I hate, as does my husband. I like us too much to put us through that!"

A healthy relationship with money is internal, unique to the beauty that is you. We all have opinions of what we should do with money, and we have different lives that require different spending decisions. Ideally we can listen to our girlfriends without judgment or jealousy as they talk about their choices and priorities around money. Lucinda, Marina and Ann, your Girlfriend Guides, often make different choices with their money. Each choice is right for that girlfriend, yet may not be right for another. We appreciate and celebrate these differences.

Optimism

The sun will come out tomorrow. It may be hidden by clouds, but it'll be there!

Lucinda's Mantra: "I have sufficient today and I am capable of taking care of myself and my family tomorrow. There might be changes. Some of these changes may be hard; however, I am capable of making change. Like bamboo, I am strong and flexible. Money is a tool to help me achieve sufficiency for my family and I can do that. Money does not define me. Therefore, a lack today or an excess tomorrow will not change who I am. I will continue to make good choices in my relationship with money."

Negative Attitudes

Just as a positive relationship with money is based on *positive* attitudes and expectations — acceptance of trade-offs, control, lack of jealousy and judgment, openness and optimism — there are common *negative* attitudes and expectations that will harm your relationship with money. Many of us carry these negative thoughts simply because we never stopped and thought about them. Luckily, once we examine them, these negative beliefs are easy enough to dispel.

These negative attitudes and expectations are:

- Feeling anxious about money.
- Thinking you need to spend a lot to belong.
- Thinking that you don't deserve good things.
- Being incompetent with money.
- Thinking that money will bring you happiness and security.
- Not understanding that there are choices.
- Spending and saving out of alignment with your values and goals.

Anxiety

"Money stresses me out!"

Almost everybody we talk to has experienced times of anxiety around money. Anxiety increases when you avoid being truly honest with yourself about your financial picture.

There was a time when Lucinda let her credit card get out of control. "The amount owing was way out of proportion to my income. I made it worse by ignoring the reality of the debt, sometimes even buying myself things to make me feel better! The worse it got, the more I hid. It was a difficult and unhappy time; I felt stressed and ashamed. Finally facing up to it was such a relief. Even though the truth wasn't pretty, I made a plan that was manageable and at last I could sleep again. I paid off that card much faster than I expected and learned the power of facing reality, no matter how ugly that reality can be."

Knowledge is power; when you know where you are financially, have goals and an action plan, your anxiety will decrease dramatically.

Belonging

"I felt horrible — I went to the dinner/dance/party and all the women were better dressed than me. I did not belong. I just wanted to go home and forget the whole thing."

A sense of belonging is critical to our sense of self worth, but it's important to understand that we belong because of who we are, not what we have. Real friends care about who you are. If you compete with your friends about who has more, then you actually have less — less girlfriends.

PS: Girlfriend, this issue of belonging is not restricted to females. Men compete just as furiously around things as do women. Their things tend to be different — they compete with tools, cars, technology and houses — but their self-worth is as tied up in money as any woman's.

Deserving

"I don't deserve peace or nice things."

"I don't deserve all the good things I have. I didn't really earn them; I just got lucky."

Unfortunately some of our girlfriends believe that they don't deserve what they have. They may say they do, but their actions say otherwise. These girlfriends regularly sabotage themselves by:

- Staying in their budget, then blowing it with a splurge.
- Not earning as much as they deserve, because they don't understand the value of their contribution.
- Not taking care of their belongings.
- Not taking care of their finances and financial future.

Consciously or not, they get rid of money as quickly as possible; anything to prove to the world and themselves that they are not worthy of the good things in life.

The foundation of any positive relationship is always how you see yourself. If you see yourself as a loser, as someone who does not have enough and is not good enough, you will attract the wrong kind of people, experiences and events. If you see yourself as out of control or unable to manage money, you will not use your money in ways that reflect your values.

Not only do you deserve things that reflect your values and desires, you also deserve the sense of peace that comes with having a great relationship with money.

Competency

"Money is complex and boring! My husband handles it all; I'm too busy with the kids to think about mortgage rates and life insurance."

"I'm horrible with money. Whatever I have seems to slip through my fingers. I can't balance a budget or control my spending."

"If I don't track my money and how I spend it, I don't have to face all the bad choices I've made. (Including that bikini.)"

As with anxiety, knowledge is power when dealing with your sense of competency. Managing your money is not difficult. The activities in this book show you that you can control your spending and make good choices. You deserve good things in life, one of which is feeling confident and capable around money.

Happiness and Security

"Money will make me happy. When I get enough, I won't be anxious or unhappy."

"Only money will bring me security, and as I don't have enough I always feel anxious."

We all feel insecure and scared at times. Money can and does make a difference in some aspects of our lives. Knowing that you can pay the rent or mortgage this month, and for the rest of the year if you had to, is a nice feeling. Being able to spoil the kids once in a while is great.

Knowing clearly and honestly where you stand financially will actually make you feel more secure, not less. As Lucinda says, "Every week when I review my bank statements, I am reminded that although I'm not a zillionaire, I'm doing OK. I feel really abundant, and proud of myself too. Even in times when money was short, when

I had to face ugly truths and make multiple trade-offs, it felt good to regain calm and control, rather than panicking and feeling terrified. There have been scary times, but you just do what you have to do, one step at a time."

How much is enough to put away and how much is obsessive? Ann used to think that having enough money would insulate her from life's catastrophes. She worked very hard to build financial security for herself and her family. In fact she worked so hard that she didn't see her family as much as she would have liked. But *that's life*, she told herself; *gotta pay off the house*. It was only after nearly losing her husband to a heart attack that she realized money in the bank could not shield her from everything. She was told he wouldn't survive; he actually died several times on that operating table. In those moments, her values shifted. Working so hard to earn money had kept her away from what was really important to her — her family. Now she works fewer hours to balance her desire for financial security with being present in her own life.

Choices

"I have options?"

"I don't have any money. I'm always in debt. Why would I need some book to fix my attitude when what I really need is more cash?"

We all have choices. Every single day we choose how we spend our money. We often lose sight of the power of these choices, which create the big picture of our relationship with money.

Some of our past choices may have been poor decisions, because making bad decisions is a part of learning and growing. We'll chalk those bad decisions up to experience and move on. But from now on we want to be careful with our decision-making around money. Each latte, each hat, each box of cookies moves us closer to, or further away from, our financial goals. No purchase is disconnected from our entire financial picture.

If getting out of debt or gaining more income is a goal, then start making choices that will lead you to that goal. Start today. Start small. Just start, one step at a time.

Spending and Saving in Alignment with Your Values

"This isn't the life I want!"

"Money is just about jobs and paying the bills. You either have enough or you don't. It has nothing to do with goals and values."

To help us consciously align our spending with our values and goals, we need to look for places where we are in conflict — where our principles collide with our actions.

For example, imagine a couple who say they need a big house because they love being home. If they have to work overtime to pay for that house, there's a conflict, because they're not home, enjoying the house. They may decide they want a smaller, less expensive house; or maybe one more conveniently located to work. Or maybe they'll decide that they are happy with their current house and are in harmony with the trade-offs they are choosing to make. Their best decision is a choice that matches their values.

Conflict can also arise when values are outdated. Our imaginary couple may realize that a big house is no longer necessary now that the kids have moved out. Perhaps they have become more environmentally aware and choose to move to a place where they can walk more than drive. After reviewing their values, our couple can make choices that fit them and their lifestyle.

...

Relationships with money are unique to each of us. While no one can tell you what values to hold, it is important that you live your life according to updated values that are truly yours. We will look at values in the next chapter.

Questions for Reflection

Gather your girlfriends or do this alone. Make a pot of tea or something stronger, and ask yourself or your friends the following questions:

- What are your negative and positive attitudes and expectations towards money?
- Growing up, what did you learn about money?
  - In your home, what was the prevailing attitude towards money? Was money scarce or abundant?
  - Who earned, used and discussed money in your home?
  - How did your parents pay for things? (cash, credit, check, debit, no idea)
  - How old were you when you started having money of your own? Did you earn money or was it given to you in the form of allowance or gifts? Were you allowed to spend it as you wanted or were there restrictions?

- o Did you have a bank account?
- o Did any particular event or set of circumstances affect your relationship with money?
- Which positive attitudes and expectations around money do you see in your friends? Your family? Your country?
- Which negative attitudes and expectations around money do you see in your friends? Family? Country?
- What's your worst money memory? Would you make the same or different choices today?
- What's your proudest money moment? Why are you so proud of it?

...

Activity: My Closet — What's in It for Me?

When it comes to our closets, most of us are somewhat unsatisfied. Many feel we lack something: the right clothes, the right fit, or the right look. Some of us think we don't have enough.

Think about how many times a day you are reminded that you need more or better. In a world full of these messages, how can you ever convince yourself that you have enough? That you have what you need and probably more?

This activity will help you access a sense of abundance in the simple context of your closet. It requires about two hours and a trusted friend. If you have a teenage daughter, they often have the loving heartlessness that this exercise calls for!

Part One

Make a list of your clothing needs for the various activities in your life. First, think of the activities you do and the clothes they require. Now write a list of the outfits you need for each activity. Everyone's list will be different.

Be sure to list what you *need* — where less would be inconvenient or inappropriate; more would be excess.

Ann's list:

- I need at least six complete work outfits. Items should be coordinated enough that I can mix and match to create two weeks' worth of office wear.
- I need two outfits for running — one to wear and one in the wash.
- I need three weekend outfits — comfortable jeans, shirts and sweaters.
- I need two fancy outfits for dinners with clients.
- I need two outfits for formal dinners or dances.
- I need all of this for both winter and summer.

Got your list? Let's move on to the second part of this activity.

Part Two

Select a trusted friend and invite her over for a Saturday afternoon. Tell her your goal, which is to feel that you have sufficient clothes and that what you have meets your needs.

1. Make a large thermos of your favorite tea or coffee and a plate of cold snacks for energy — you'll need them!

2. Clean up your bedroom and set out a table and chair for your friend.

3. Then take everything — and we mean everything! — out of your closet and pile it on your bed. Make separate piles of sweaters, suits, skirts, shirts, pants etc.

4. Show your friend your list of clothing needs, and pick a category — say work clothes. Invite your friend to go through the piles and pick a few items of work clothes from each pile. Ask her to choose the items she thinks look best on you. If you instantly agree check the outfit off your list, place it back in your closet and move on to the next one. If you disagree — think it is not your best — ask your friend why she liked it so much on you. You might be pleasantly surprised! Keep going until you have all your outfits for this category.

5. Move on to the next area of your list — for example, weekend wear. Keep going until all the categories are completed.

6. Look at what is left on the bed. Can you make another outfit? If you can, make another outfit for each category.

7. If there is a special thing left on the bed, something that you really want to keep, then keep it. But recognize that it is excess — over and above your needs and wants!

The Leftovers

Everything left on the bed is excess. You have more than you can use. This is where your friend's honesty comes in — are those items there because they don't look that great on you?

Ann had a favorite grey skirt. "I wore it all weekend every weekend, because it was really comfortable and I thought it looked good. A girlfriend took me aside and said: 'That skirt does not flatter your figure. You have a great set of legs and it hides them. You are more than that skirt, and because you wear it so often we don't get to see the other clothes you have that really flatter you.' That skirt had to go!"

Take everything left on the bed, including the clothes that you and your friend agree don't flatter you, and put them in a pile to give away or sell. We suggest a give-away pile because we feel so good about having more than enough, and like to share our bounty with others. If you are a seller, try selling them on eBay, a garage sale, or a consignment shop. If you like hosting parties, organize a clothes swap: it's a fun way to show off your clean and organized closet and, more important, share your newfound abundance skills. Lucinda donates her excess to a local women's shelter where the residents need good clothes for job interviews.

Ann gives away her excess, but before doing so, she piles it on top of an armoire in her bedroom. She says, "I can see that armoire from my bed. At night I look at the pile and think about how much I have. I have more than enough. I have excess. Before I go shopping I look at that pile and ask myself if what I buy today will end up there."

Ann's method works for her — very neat people would find it difficult! — because it reminds her to pause and reflect when caught up in a shopping high. It reminds her that even those seemingly most desirable items lose their luster over time once the thrill wears off. (Kind of like Lucinda's first boyfriend!) And then it's just painful getting rid of them.

Marina, on the other hand, gets her excess out of the house right away. "It goes into the car in bags. Next time I'm out driving, I stop at the first charity donation box I see and dump it all in. Done and done."

When you limit the number of items in your closet, if something new comes in, something older must go out. Next time you are clothes shopping, ask yourself these three questions:
- *What does this item improve on?*
- *Is it better than what I already have?*
- *What am I willing to give up for this?*

Questions for Reflection

- How did I feel doing The Closet exercise?
- What surprised me? Depressed me? Embarrassed me?
- Can I apply this exercise to other areas of my life?
- What are my plans for my excess?
- How will this change the way I shop?
- What makes me feel rich? That I have abundance and live well?
- What tells me I am poor? That what I have is not enough or not good enough?

2. Establishing Your Values

Getting to the Heart of the Matter

Having the right attitude and expectations is only the foundation of a positive relationship with money. The most important part of being successful with money is being sure that you earn, spend and save your money according to your values. **When your spending is in alignment with your values, you will feel abundant and fulfilled**.

What are Values?

Your values are the most important things in your life. They are the things that make you happy and drive your life.

Unique

Your values are uniquely yours — part of who you are. Like fingerprints, they are **unique**. Unlike fingerprints, our values often **evolve** and change over the course of our lifetime. Your definition of family may change, or where you want to live, or work.

Values are **neither right nor wrong**. Lucinda, for example, values time alone. She knows she has to give up some activities and types of employment so that she can have time for writing and to recharge. She knows that when she lives out of alignment with her values her mental and physical health suffer. (Her kids agree!) Her need for alone time is neither good nor bad; it just is. Another person may hate spending time alone. Whose values are right? Each person's — for themselves.

Non-negotiable

Most values are **non-negotiable**, which is why we experience gut-wrenching stress when we live out of alignment with our values, or when our values collide.

Ann values financial security. Another value of hers is meaningful work. Several years ago, she quit her full-time job to start a consulting company. Although it felt more meaningful, working for herself required her to give up what she perceived as financial security, and to redefine it. She went through a period of serious angst and disharmony until she could resolve the conflict of her values.

Define your Values

What motivates you? How do you wish to live? What do you believe in? What tells you that your life is successful? What do you want more of? Less of? Since every use of your money supports something, what do **you** want to support?

Clearly and consciously **defining your values** is important. After defining your values, you are then able to set financial goals that will support these values, helping you live your life consistently, calmly and with direction.

You know you've got a handle on your values when you can state them in a clear and simple way. Ann defines her values as:

- Family — togetherness, raising a healthy and happy child.
- Community — being a good, dependable friend.
- Financial Security — for taking care of my family and community.

Define your Terms

Be clear, not only in your value statement, but in what you mean by it. The words that Ann uses could mean vastly different things to each of us. Ann's definition of family means husband, child, and a small, tight-knit community. Marina's definition of family is broader, including a large extended family, and whoever her brothers are dating this week.

You also have to clarify what it is about each value that is important to you. What does family mean to you: Is it spending time together daily or only on special occasions? What do you do when you're together? Do you value being able to support your family financially, or spiritually and emotionally? Does any of that have an expiry date, such as when they move out or get married?

Are these Values Really Mine?

In the process of defining and clarifying your values, you may discover that you have been carrying other people's values — values you don't really believe in. You may have acquired them growing up, or later from friends and society. Revisiting your values allows you to maintain those you still believe in, and discard the others.

Lucinda was a non-traveler in a family of travelers. "They would tell me I should save up and see the world, but I never seemed to get the money together. One day I realized that travel is just not something I hold as a core value. It's not that I can't manage my money; it's that I was spending and saving in alignment with my core values. No wonder I always had money for other things but never for travel."

Now it's time to get clear on what's important to you. **You**. Not advertisers, your friends or family. This is your life; let's get started on making it fabulous.

Activity: What are my Values?

In this activity we want you to state your values. What is most important to you? What is your purpose in life; your mission statement? How do you like to live?

Remember that these are your values — no one else's. These are not values you think you should have, like pretending to value spending time with family when you secretly hate them. This is about what you really want and what excites you. Pay attention to any positive feelings or warm memories that arise as you work through this; they will guide you to what you hold most important.

- List your values.
- Be as brief or wordy as you want.

Look for conflicts

Now find a girlfriend or two. Ask your friends to point out any conflicts between what you say and do. For example, you may claim to value health and fitness but smoke like a fiend and live on junk food. This would be a conflict and you would need to change either the value statement or your actions.

...

Now you know your core values. You know what you want and what's important to you. Hold on to this list — you'll use it again in the following chapters.

3. Creating your Financial Goals and Action Plans

After defining your values, you are now ready to create your **financial goals**. Financial goals are what you work towards. Broken down into clear, achievable milestones, goals steer your life, helping with daily decisions and long-term directional choices.

Good financial goals are **deeply personal**. They reflect your story and how you want to grow. Financial goals must be right for *you* — it's difficult to meet goals that feel foreign or imposed. When your financial goals are based on your values — what is most important to you — you are more likely to stay on course, and to succeed just by being yourself.

Goals must be **clearly defined**. *Being rich* is not a valid goal because it's too vague. You'd have to define what *being rich* means to you. What would it look like? Would it be a certain bank balance? Paying off your house or driving a fancy car? Knowing that you could get a job anywhere, or that you have friends and family who would help if you had a financial crisis? The answer(s) would be your financial goals.

Goals must be **achievable** as a result of your actions. *Winning the lottery*, for example, is not a valid goal because it is not within your control; buying tickets is as far as you can take it.

Goals are **measureable**. Did I achieve this goal? Is it 100% complete? Did I do it within my timeline?

As with values, goals must be **consciously reviewed** and **re-evaluated regularly**. Goals should be monitored and assessed, then updated and adjusted as necessary.

…

Ann's financial goals come from values she developed as a result of two defining episodes early in her life. "The first was being adopted as a toddler. Although I have few memories of that time, I have an enduring sense of loss and insecurity. The second episode was a few years later, when a close friend had to move away because her family could no longer afford their house. I missed my friend so much! I vowed that I would always have enough money to prevent valuable relationships being taken away from me.

"As an adult setting my financial goals, I recognized that I value security. I then defined a couple of financial goals that would help me feel more secure:

1. Create a financial safety net based on my own abilities, skills and knowledge. For me that meant funding my education, getting a degree in my field of expertise and staying current. I budget 5% of my income to education each year.

2. Save enough money to last six months if I lost my job or could not work, by putting aside 5% of my income until I reached the balance I wanted."

…

Activity: My Financial Goals

It's time for you to set your financial goals. For this activity, try to come up with between three and five financial goals to support your core values.

1. Look at your list of values that you made in Chapter 2.
2. What are the financial goals that would support those values? Write them down.
3. After you have listed your financial goals, take another look:
   - Do your financial goals **match your values**? Do you believe in them?
   - Are they written in such a way that they have meaning to you? Are you excited and maybe even a little bit scared? Do they fit like a great pair of jeans?
   - Are your intentions **clear** and **measurable**? How will you know when you have achieved a goal? Be specific — what does it look like, smell like, feel like? How is your life different?
4. List the trade-offs required. Are you willing to make those compromises? Are there alternatives?

…

Action Plans

Goals are where you want to go. Action plans help you get there. A good action plan becomes a clear set of steps toward your goal and is your roadmap to success.

Action plans are made by breaking down the goal into smaller pieces called milestones. The financial goal of *home ownership* can be broken down into these milestones:

- Create the income that allows you to afford the house. You can break this down into sub-milestones such as:
  - identifying work that pays in the range of your target income
  - funding and getting the training or education you require
  - developing your resume
  - finding employment
- Research where you want to live
- Research real estate — the local market, laws, procedures and processes
- Shop around for mortgages

After listing your milestones, estimate how long each item will take, and decide when it should start and complete. These dates become your timeline.

How to Create an Action Plan

1. **Set a clear intention**. State your financial goal.
2. Create a **timeline**. Set a deadline then work backwards,

dividing the process into achievable milestones with realistic deadlines.

3. **Track your progress**. You have to know where you are successful and where you need to change course slightly. Expect to change course occasionally — as we know better, we do better.

Marina's House

Marina lives in a big, beautiful, old house. Like most older homes it requires a lot of maintenance — current estimates are about $200,000 for the necessary structural repairs and system upgrades. That does not include renovations or fun stuff.

The house and yard are so large that to care for them is more than a fulltime job. Marina did try to handle it in addition to work, school, and parenting but it was too much. With age comes wisdom, and Marina discovered that she had options. After she revisited her values, she set new financial goals.

Marina listed her values as:

- Time with family
- "Me" time
- Financial independence
- Lifelong learning

One of Marina's values is financial independence. She chose the following financial goals to support that value:

- Sell my house and move to a less resource-sucking one.
- Create one or more sources of passive income.
- Increase my employment income.

After evaluating her financial goals, Marina chose to focus on selling the house first. Doing so will facilitate her other financial goals: the new home will include a rental suite, creating passive income; and living in a home that requires less time to maintain will free up time for Marina to go back to school in order to increase her employment income.

Marina then looked at what trade-offs are required, and began to list possible solutions. The trade-offs required to sell her house are:

- Letting go of the "dream house" and getting real about what works for me.
- Space. A smaller house will probably have less space. Possible compromises are to de-junk and investigate storage solutions. Less space may conflict with my "Me time" value, because it might be harder to find a quiet place to hide out in.
- The work required to prepare the house for sale. Can I give myself enough time and/or get help?
- The hassle of moving (ack!). I'll help the kids prepare mentally and physically. I'll ensure enough time for packing and unpacking, and a weekend trip to the local spa resort with my girlfriends afterwards.
- Needing to negotiate a new mortgage — will I get the same great rate? I will research rates and policies.

Knowing her first financial goal, Marina then went to work to create her action plan.

1. Set a Clear Intention

- I want to sell this house for $X, buy another house for $Y and invest the difference, or carry a smaller mortgage.
- I visualize living in a house that fits my family and lifestyle. The new house must-haves include: three bedrooms, eat-in kitchen, sunny yard, mudroom, garage, two bathrooms, in our current neighborhood, rental suite.

2. Create a Timeline

I want to place the house on the market 10 months from now. In that time, as well as meeting my normal obligations, I need to do my taxes (to have my finances in order when applying for the new mortgage), clean and de-clutter the house, and have the property appraised by a realtor. The realtor will give me a list of tasks to prepare the property for sale. I expect those tasks to take about three months to complete.

Counting backwards from my deadline of 10 months, I estimated how long each milestone will take, then created a timeline:

1 month from now: Do taxes
3 months from now: Clean and declutter (will take about 3 months)
4 months from now: Property value appraisal
5 months from now: Deal with realtor's to-do list (will take about 4 months)
9 months from now: Open house
10 months from now: Sell house
11 months from now: Reinvest the profits (and spa trip!)

3. Track Progress and Adjust as Necessary

After making the timeline, I can add secondary items such as finding my new home and researching investment opportunities. I will track my progress and adjust the timeline or expectations as necessary.

...

Financial goals are:

- A result of your values
- Deeply personal. You succeed just by being yourself.
- Clearly defined
- Consciously reviewed and re-evaluated regularly
- Achievable as a result of your actions. They are within your control.
- Measureable — what by when?

How to create an action plan

1. Set a clear intention — your financial goal.
2. Create a timeline and divide it into milestones.
3. Track your progress and adjust milestones as necessary.

Now you know your values, financial goals and how to create an action plan for each goal. You have created a map of what's important to you and how you are going to get it.

Yay — that was the hardest part! It's all fun and shopping from here ...

4. Spending according to your Values

Many of us think we are incompetent with money, but actually the opposite is true: we are extremely competent in our spending.

We are good at it but rarely are we thoughtful about it. A key step to having a great relationship with money is to look at your spending habits compared to your values.

What you buy has little to do with happiness, fulfillment and joy. No matter how much you buy, it won't make you happy.

We are not saying don't buy. We are saying that buying aimlessly and endlessly will not fill you up. There is nothing wrong with upgrading your wardrobe, but shopping without knowing what you really want will not improve the quality of your life — in fact, it will make it worse.

Shop mindfully.
Shop with a purpose.
Shop to improve your quality of life —
not the amount of stuff you own.
Control waste.

Does your Spending Support your Values?

Lucinda's values are:
- Physical and Spiritual Fitness
- Family
- Work

Looking at her spending, she listed her top ten expenses, and checked that each one supports one or more of her values.

Expense	Value that is supported
1. Taxes	Staying out of jail
2. Housing	Physical and Spiritual Fitness, Family
3. Food	Physical and Spiritual Fitness, Family
4. Transportation	Work
5. Activities and Lessons	Physical and Spiritual Fitness
6. Insurance	Physical and Spiritual Fitness
7. Clothes	Family
8. Long term savings	Family
9. Education	Work
10. Business Development	Work

If she noticed that one of her expenses did not align with a value, she could make changes to realign her spending.

Activity: But Back to Me ...

Make a list of your top ten expenses and which of your values they support. Remember your expenses and values will be different from Lucinda's; you are unique and so is your spending.

My Top Ten Expenses

Expense	Value that is supported
1.	
2.	
3.	
4.	
5.	
6.	
7.	
8.	
9.	
10.	

Does your spending support your values? Are you surprised which values you spend the most on? Or the least?

Are You Spending Effectively?

Do you get the most out of your money? Do you spend *effectively*? Are there lower-priced alternatives that would still support your values but allow you to save money?

Lucinda made a chart of her spending to support each value, and some lower-priced alternatives that would still satisfy that value. Here's her chart on the value of family.

Value: Family	
Spending	**Lower Priced Alternatives**
Arts and sports lessons and equipment	Lessons only for what they really want Buy used sport equipment
Outings and entertaining	Do free activities together such as cycling, jogging, cooking, gardening
Kids' college funds	Ask relatives for college fund donations instead of gifts
Vacations	"Staycations" and shorter vacations

Activity: Bang for my Buck

Try to come up with at least three lower-priced alternatives that would still satisfy each of your values while saving you money.

Value:	
Spending	**Lower Priced Alternatives**

There are more Bang for my Buck blank templates available on our website at GirlfriendsGuideToMoney.com

A Note on False Economies

Are there places where you might be shortchanging yourself — making false economies — by saving in areas that might have better payback?

We're not saying blow the budget. You have to align your finances with reality, but also remember that we need to live, learn and grow. There are things and priorities on which we should spend money. Lucinda has a great example:

"For a while in my life, I was a (mostly) stay-at-home mom with young kids and a big dog. My life was as unglamorous as my rubber boots. If the kids didn't cover me in food or markers, the dog would manage to fling mud on me. My wardrobe needs centered around warm, washable and comfortable.

"Because I brought in very little money I didn't feel right spending much on clothes or shoes, so I bought cheap shoes at discount stores. I walked a lot and was heavier then, so I went through several pairs a year. One day I realized I had actually spent *more* money buying many pairs of cheap shoes than if I had bought one or two more expensive but well-made pairs. I was paying *more* for discomfort and poor support! Now I buy well-priced AND well-made shoes. That's not to say I don't look for a good deal. But I have learned that cheaper is not necessarily less expensive."

Look at your spending through a different lens now, asking if you should be spending **more** money somewhere. If you're like Ann and don't spend enough on work clothes, this can actually be a license to shop!

Why Do You Purchase What You Do?

As you become more aware of your spending compared to your values, you may see inconsistencies; that you are spending on the wrong thing. With awareness you may see that you are attempting to solve a deeper or different problem.

Ann looked at two of her spending habits. "One is going for coffee by myself at work — driving to the coffee shop and having a six dollar coffee and muffin when I am stressed. I like to go out because in my job it's very hard to get time alone.

"Another spending habit I reviewed is buying lots of things for my daughter. I like to do that because she's a good kid and deserves it. When I was a kid I never got the cool or fashionable stuff and hated not having what my friends had. I want my daughter to feel part of her group.

"But neither of these spending habits align with my values. So I looked for alternatives that are more aligned with my values. Here's what I came up with:

1. Going for coffee
Why: To get time alone.
Lower-priced alternative that meets my values: I could go for a walk, which would also be healthier.

2. Buying lots of stuff for my daughter
Why: I like to spoil my daughter and I want her to fit in by having the stuff her friends have.
Lower-priced alternatives that meet my values: Remember that what my daughter wants is me, not things. Get her to write a list of

things she wants and then help her to earn money by doing some work *with* me.

Each of these lower-priced alternatives fits my values and is easy enough to do. But I wasn't doing either of them. I had to stop and ask myself what stops me from doing those alternatives?

1. Going for a walk instead of coffee
Stoppage: I hate the cold and the damp (and I live in the Pacific Northwest!)

2. Working with my daughter to help her earn money, instead of just buying stuff
Stoppage: Is this how I want to spend my free time — doing chores?

Now that I know my stoppages, I can solve them. How can I fix those stoppages?

1. Going for a walk instead of coffee
Stoppage: Hating the cold and rain
Solution: My office has a gym; I could get alone time if I walked on the treadmill.

2. Working with my daughter to help her earn money, instead of just buying stuff
Stoppage: Not wanting to spend my free time doing chores
Solution: I am doing laundry and dishes anyhow — I could do them with my daughter. I have an awesome picture of my family doing dishes when I was a kid. I will put it on the fridge to remind me what great times you can have, even doing 'boring' things."

Activity: Why am I Spending?

Now it's your turn. Pick two or three expenditures as examples.

1. List the expenditures and why you make them.
2. Are there lower-cost alternatives that still meet your values?
3. What would stop you from using those alternatives?
4. Are there solutions to those stoppages?

Remember, there are no right answers — only the answers that are right for you.

Expenditure	
Why I make it	
Lower-priced alternatives	
Stoppages	
Solutions to the stoppages	

There are more Why Am I Spending blank templates available on our website at GirlfriendsGuideToMoney.com.

Daily Spending

You make daily decisions that affect your finances. When it comes to smaller purchases, what's your method for determining what you do and don't spend money on? Do you just go with your mood, or do you have established rules for spending?

One of Lucinda's favorite and most successful practices is The List. Not just any list: *The List*.

Rules of The List
Buy all that is on The List.
Buy only that which is on The List.
The List rules all.

As a concept, The List is stupidly easy. Putting in into practice is also easy. It requires no special tools or skills, is portable and free.

Here's how it works:

Post a list somewhere you can see it. Ours is scrap paper held together by a clip that hangs from a thumbtack. Like I said, no special tools!

On The List goes everything to be bought. Groceries usually account for most of it; the rest is comprised of things for the house or garden, kids' clothing, or stuff someone needs for a party or school project.

When kids ask for something, I tell them to write it on The List. When I go shopping, I take The List.

With The List shopping is easy. If it's on The List you may purchase it. If it's not on The List, you don't purchase it. You never have to make an on-the-spot decision about whether to buy a thing. (On-the-spot spending decisions are rarely aligned with your goals and values, and leaking money on spontaneous, unnecessary expenditures is a sure route to financial disability.)

When you use The List at the grocery store, you no longer accidentally buy eight boxes of cookies because you were hungry or tired.

According to the rules of The List, when you're in your favorite great-deals-on-clothing-and-housewares store and you see a gorgeous, green vase that practically glows and makes you funny in the knees, you don't buy it unless you have the words "Vase, Shiny Green Decoration," or "Large Breakable Item" on your List.

You won't buy it today, but here's the secret of The List: you *can* buy that thing you suddenly think you can't live without. Go home and add the vase to your List. Decide when to purchase it, appropriate to your budget. You can look forward to buying it, imagining how glamorous life will become once you have it. You will start to experience owning that vase.

The next time you're in the store, you can buy that vase. But what often happens is that when you see it again, some of the luster has worn off; you're not quite as enamored. The simple act of indulging in desire turns out to be its own payoff.

You may decide not to buy the item, or to wait another week to see if you really, really want it.

What if, when you return to the store, you love the item just as much if not more? Then whoopee, you know it's a good purchase for you! You know that you are buying something you love.

With The List you still get to treat yourself (always in proportion to your budget). In fact you pamper yourself because you eliminate bad-purchase guilt, and buy things that you truly love.

The List enables me to be a wise shopper without having to invoke willpower in the face of shiny things. It's saved me probably thousands of dollars — and more important, millions of calories

— in the three years since I initiated it. It will save me thousands more.

Spending Wisely

Buy what you want your life to grow into

Lucinda says, "I decided I wanted to live a life that required or included kick-ass professional clothes. I bought a few simple basics to start: black pants, grey pants, two dressy (for me) blouses, a camisole, and a blazer. As I grew comfortable with the idea of seeing myself dressed well, I bought a couple of jackets, some good shoes, and finally some coats. I didn't rush myself or create stress by doing it all at once. I allowed myself the time to grow into a higher version of myself. Had I tried to do it all at once, I would have gotten scared and failed."

Buy what you love

We've all made bad purchases: shoes that a friend talked us into buying, a great shirt that doesn't fit well, pants that don't go with anything. Each item is perfectly good, and some may have been expensive, but you just never wear them. Every time you open your closet you get a reminder of wasted money. When you buy less and only what you love, you may have fewer items in your closet or kitchen, but each item will be a favorite!

Buy what you want

What is it that you want? You, not your friends or family. If you don't like gourmet meals, then fancy restaurants are wasted money. If you don't read them, cancel the highbrow subscriptions that are supposed to impress your visitors. Be sure to spend your limited resources in alignment with your own values.

Reward yourself

Build rewards into your budget. Make them proportionate to your budget; if you have lots of money, take a vacation every three months; if you have just a little, go to a museum or park. Pampering yourself can be as simple and inexpensive as a hot bath or a slow, mindful facial or even a seat in the sunshine. It can be listening to uplifting music or buying yourself an ice cream. Lucinda says, "I reward myself every day and every week. I always feel pampered."

...

You've done it! You have taken a mirror to your values and looked at your spending as a reflection of those values. That wasn't too hard or painful, was it?

Now you know how you want to spend your money. You know where you want your money to go. Your spending reflects the beautiful person you are.

5. Building a Strong Support Network

As the old saying goes, the only constant in life is change. Some life changes require you to reassess where you are financially. Whenever your life path takes a major change, you may need the support of your best girlfriends to help you through it.

Ann, Lucinda and Marina spent a lot of time together during the writing of this book, sharing stories and defining our values, goals and action plans. Whenever we talked about financial hard times, a common comment was *If only I'd known there were people who offer this kind of help! I'd have solved my problem that much faster, and probably saved myself from all this grey hair.*

Everyone goes through hard times, but no one has to do it alone. If you create a strong network of friends and professionals, and turn to them in your time of need, you increase your chances of success and decrease your amount of stress.

We know that sometimes it's hard to reach out for help. Each of us has experienced the fear and anxiety of struggling alone through a vital yet unfamiliar process. Each of us has also learned the joys of working with a professional who not only knows things we don't, but also has great connections and up to date information on their area of expertise.

Part of a successful financial strategy is building a strong team around you to support, lead and teach you. Having someone on your side takes a lot of stress out of an already tense time in your life. You still have to go through it, but this may help you sleep at night.

Although we like to act like we know everything, we don't. (Just ask our kids!) There are times in your life when you will need specific advice and information from experts, so we've invited a few Expert Girlfriends (not all of whom are excited by that title, especially the men) to contribute their expertise.

Our Expert Girlfriends and the companies they represent are outstanding in their fields. Each has contributed a chapter (except our overachiever Greg, who contributed two) about their field of expertise. Topics include:

- Oh no! Insurance?!
- Is bankruptcy the right choice for me?
- When you need someone to talk to at work.
- When you're leaving a job
- I've been fired! What do I do now?
- When you're looking for a job.
- Just got that dream job!

Many of these topics are job-related because for many of us, employment income is our main source of money. We want you to know what resources are out there, who can help you and where to start.

We wish you the best and now turn you over to some of our favorite experts …

6. Oh No, Insurance?!

By Paul Stephens

Insurance is one of those topics that you may relate to as ABCD: Absolutely Atrocious, Bitterly Boring, Completely Confusing, and Dully Depressing. You are not alone. You might know that insurance is something important to consider in your financial life, but it seems so complicated and involves all those scary, sad things that might happen to you and your family and home.

It's OK! You're with your girlfriends and it's safe to talk about this. Be brave for yourself, your kids and your family. Reading about these things and thinking about scary events doesn't mean they will happen. And arming yourself with some knowledge may be your best protection and give you peace of mind.

"What is it?"

Insurance is a bit like a big pot of money where everyone tosses in some cash on a regular basis (called premiums). If something unpredicted happens, you get to take some cash out (called benefits or settlements). The unpredicted event might be your house burning down (for house insurance), a car accident (for car insurance), or a death within the next year (one year term life insurance). The idea is that people who are exposed to these risks and are interested in protecting themselves against them, will be willing to pay into these plans. The risks are generally things that are out of our control, that (if they were to occur) would have a personal, significant financial impact.

Insurance is most commonly used to protect your significant assets against the risks they face. We hear you — it's kind of depressing, because many of the risks are things we just don't want to think about, like dying or getting sick. Some common examples of insurance might help you to relate a bit better.

Property insurance: If your house was destroyed or significantly damaged, it would be very costly to repair or replace it. Even if you rent an apartment, if your home was destroyed, imagine the devastating costs of replacing all your clothes, furniture and belongings.

Car insurance: Imagine the cost if your car was damaged or stolen, if you had an accident that damaged property, or if you hurt someone while driving. Vehicle insurance is mandatory for most drivers.

Life and accident insurance: Everyone dies eventually, but there would be an enormous impact if you died or were severely injured while you were still working and you had a family that was financially dependent upon you. Or perhaps you want to leave some money behind to cover things such as funeral expenses, debts or taxes.

Disability insurance: If you got sick and could not work for a prolonged period of time, how would you pay your rent, mortgage, or credit card bills? Did you know that working women are more likely than men to have a medical condition giving rise to a work-disrupting disability?

Health insurance: The costs of medical incidents can be huge and unforeseen. Imagine you have an accident while vacationing in a foreign country and you had to be hospitalized and have an operation! What if you were diagnosed at home with an illness for which a costly medication was required? Or what if your child needs costly dental work? Health and dental insurance is a popular form of insurance you may have heard of.

"Is everything insurable?"

Spilling red wine on your favorite white dress before that big party might seem like a huge calamity, but it's probably not something you can insure yourself against (unless perhaps you are royalty!) Not every risk would have a significant financial impact, or is of interest to enough people to warrant selling policies.

"Why do insurance companies ask you questions?"

Sometimes insurers want to check things before they agree to insure you or your possessions. They might ask to inspect you or your possessions. They do this for many reasons. For example, they want to make sure the items actually exist, are in decent shape and aren't already suffering from an issue that might automatically give rise to a claim immediately or soon after starting the insurance. If they ask to have a look and you decline, this would stop the process. Similarly, if they inspect your health and find something they don't like, they may decline to cover you.

Like credit bureaus, insurance companies keep a central record of applications for certain types of insurance. Why? It helps to prevent them insuring the same thing multiple times unnecessarily, and flags people who may have questionable health or insurance shopping tactics. These approaches are all geared at trying to ensure the event being insured is as unpredictable to the insurer as it is to the person buying the insurance.

Another way insurance companies try to keep events equally unpredictable to both you and them is to allow a policy to be sold, but have certain things that are excluded. It's really important to understand what types of exclusions your insurance contains. For example, house insurance policies would exclude the scenario of you burning down your own house for the pay out. In medical and disability policies, sometimes there are "pre-existing conditions" exclusions. This means that if you already had a certain disease, say cancer, that you were treated for shortly before the policy was issued, then you could claim for other types of diseases and events, but claims concerning cancer would be excluded.

Remember when filling in paperwork with insurance companies, it's very important to answer questions truthfully: to do otherwise could make your claim ineligible. It's also very important to understand what is included and excluded in the policy you are buying. Never be afraid to ask for more information or to have something explained again until you understand it.

As you get older you are more likely to develop medical conditions that would prevent you from being eligible for insurance, or would limit your options. It's often best to think about your insurance options as early as you can in life, consider how your needs might change over time, and revisit your plan periodically to make sure it still meets the needs you had planned for.

"But the government will take care of me, right?"

This is a common misconception. Many countries have a variety of public systems to provide some degree of coverage to some or all of the population. For example, it might cover hospitals and doctors, or it might cover medications for low income seniors. It might be a payout in the event of death, or payments to cover lost income in the event of work interruptions. Some jurisdictions have quasi-public agencies to cover the costs associated with certain on-the-job work-related illnesses, accidents and deaths. The complex system in most western countries leaves many people with the sense that we'll be taken care of, but it may surprise you that many things are in fact not covered by these programs. Many programs have been facing great financial strains and cutbacks. While these public programs may provide a basic amount of coverage to certain people, you may decide that the needs of you and your family require more income.

"I'm just a regular person — isn't insurance for people with valuables?"

When you consider the cost of replacing the things you own, the potential financial impact of an untimely death, or the expenses of a prolonged illness, you might see that insurance could play a useful role in protecting your future. Make a list of the things you own and the monthly costs that your family would have if your income was no longer coming in.

"Insurance companies just want my money — I will never see a dime!"

Insurers have a contract that requires them to pay you if the event happens. If they didn't pay up, word would get out and people would stop buying their policies. There are also regulators in many countries that watch over these issues. Don't buy anything if you don't fully understand what is covered and what is not covered. Ask questions until you understand and read materials carefully.

"Where do I buy it?"

Insurance is sold in many places these days. On the internet, from salespeople (sometimes called "agents" or "brokers"), over the phone, and in shopping malls. Look for trusted agents, brokers, and insurance companies with a good track record and good finances. Ask your friends or family for referrals if they have insurance themselves. Interview the broker. Remember you are in control of your plans and don't feel pressured to buy. Ask lots of questions: taking notes can be helpful to some people, so carry a pen and notebook with you.

"I don't have any insurance … do I?"

Don't despair over the insurance situation. You may not be as exposed as you might think. Here are some places you might check out:

- You likely have some protection from public programs in your area that you qualify for. You might check online or call your government offices locally to understand a bit about unemployment insurance, disability, workers compensation, medical, and death benefits.
- If you have loans such as a mortgage or credit cards, you might have insurance if you were to die or become disabled. Give them a call.
- If you are employed, you might also have access to group insurance. Group insurance is most commonly provided by employers, unions, trade associations, and other groups. More about this below. Ask your Human Resources department, union representative, or association representative if you have coverage available and if you are eligible. If so, ask for a copy of the booklet describing the coverage and any forms you are required to fill out.

"What is group insurance?"

Group insurance is sometimes called "employee benefits plans" or "group benefits." Group insurance covers a whole bunch of people at once under one insurance policy. One entity (say an employer company) agrees to cover the premium bill each month, and manages the paperwork with the insurance company. Policies may have different sets of eligibility and waiting requirements for different pieces of the plan.

Your group plan might require you to pay for some of the costs from each pay check; however the costs of group plans are generally lower than the costs of individual plans, or they might offer better coverage than you could purchase on your own. Since many union plans and employer-sponsored plans are at no cost or partial cost to you, these plans can be an often under-appreciated and overlooked perk.

When you are eligible to join the plan, you will be asked to fill in an application form and other paperwork. No one likes paperwork, but don't give up! Filling it in won't take long. If you need help, ask for it from your Human Resources department or union representative, or call the insurance company. Make sure you enroll yourself and your family members if they are eligible, but ensure you understand the costs of the plan for you and your family.

The most common types of protection include health and dental, life insurance and perhaps disability. Usually it provides you with some fundamental amount of insurance protection, but without the insurer needing to ask to research you and your health. Some plans allow you to obtain extra levels of coverage if you pass their medical screening; for example you might be able to get additional life insurance at an additional cost if you pass the insurance company's health screening tests.

Some plans might or might not give you the option to pass up the coverage for all or some of the coverage. For example, you might already have health coverage for yourself and children under your spouse's plan that you think is enough for your needs. If this was the case, and it was permitted, you would sign an agreement to waive the health coverage under your plan for the reason you already have a similar plan. You need to be very careful about doing this. Some plans have an "all-or-nothing" approach so waiving health coverage might mean you do not get the life insurance or disability coverage either. You should also ask whether you can get into the plan at a later date should your spouse's plan cease if, for example, they lost their job. Some plans might have medical screening requirements if you apply later on. Check your plan and your spouse's carefully to understand how the plans can work together — or not. Many policies allow you to be covered under both policies, but some do not.

Group insurance usually stays in place only while you are an employee or an eligible member of the group, so it's important to think about this when you make a change that might disrupt this coverage, such as quitting or working reduced hours. Some programs also continue some coverage for those who retire while in the group plan, under certain conditions. Many jurisdictions allow you to buy some level of individual (non-group) coverage within a specific timeframe if you lose coverage. This access is generally without requirement for medical screening if you apply within the timeframes. For example you might be able to get some level of life insurance or some amount of health coverage if you lose your job and apply within 31 days to have your own independent policy.

...

About the Author: Paul Stephens

Paul Stephens,
Manager, Group Client
Development Pacific
Blue Cross

Paul has been in the group benefits industry for over 20 years and has worked with Pacific Blue Cross both as an Account Manager and a Manager. Prior to working at PBC, Paul worked in the field of group benefits consulting and brokerage.

Paul's career in the benefit industry has included pension and benefit plan consulting with specialization in the design and implementation of benefit plans, flexible benefit plans, multi-divisional plan management, multi-employer plans, and union plans.

Paul is a graduate of the University of British Columbia (B.Sc. Math), and is an Associate of the Society of Actuaries. He currently holds a Certified Employee Benefits Specialist (CEBS) designation and is licensed in British Columbia for life insurance sales. He is currently a member of the Canadian Pension & Benefits Institute.

Paul would like to thank the leadership team at PBC / BC Life for their support, and in particular to acknowledge the following individuals for their contributions to this chapter:

Anne Kinvig, Chief Operating Officer
Morris Nord, Senior Vice President Marketing
Brian Mathae, Director Group Client Development
Lucette Wesley, Director BC Life Claims Services
Heather Biddell, Manager BC Life Claims Services

About Pacific Blue Cross

Pacific Blue Cross has been British Columbia's leading benefits provider for over 70 years. Our comprehensive understanding of health care fuels our commitment to service. Together with BC Life, our subsidiary, we provide health, dental, life, disability and travel coverage for approximately 1.5 million British Columbians through employee group plans and through individual plans for those who do not have coverage with their employer. Pacific Blue Cross and BC Life continue to respond to customers' needs in plan design, administration and technology.

www.pac.bluecross.ca

7. Is Bankruptcy the Right Choice for Me?

By Blair Mantin

A girlfriend comes to me for advice. Here is how our conversation might go:

"I feel overwhelmed by my debts. All I'm able to do is make the minimum payments on my balances and I don't seem to be getting ahead. Now, I'm receiving harassing phone calls several times a day and I don't know what to do. What are my options?"

You have a number of options to consider when figuring out how to deal with an unmanageable debt burden. The main thing to keep in mind is that you are not alone. In 2010, more than 140,000 Canadians sought relief from their debts by either declaring personal bankruptcy or by making a Consumer Proposal.

"I definitely don't want to go bankrupt! I've never heard of a Consumer Proposal before — how does it work?"

The fastest growing alternative to bankruptcy is what's known as a Consumer Proposal. Of the 140,000 people who sought help last year, nearly 30% of them opted to file a Consumer Proposal instead of going bankrupt.

Whereas a bankruptcy consists of you essentially throwing up your hands and declaring a ceasefire, a Consumer Proposal consists of a "deal" you work out with your creditors to negotiate a reduced amount of payments over a period of time, with no more interest accruing on your debts.

For example, let's say you have debts of $20,000 in total and are unable to keep up with the payments. You would sit down with a Trustee in Bankruptcy to review your options. The Trustee would consider your monthly income in determining what a proposal might look like. A good starting point would be to look at what monthly payment you could afford, over what period of time (by law, a Consumer Proposal cannot extend past five years). You and the Trustee might determine that you could afford to pay approximately $170 per month, over the next three years, which would result in you paying back approximately 30% of your total debt.

The Trustee would then compare this result to a bankruptcy to determine what your payment would be if you went bankrupt, and how much of your debts your creditors might recover. Provided that the Consumer Proposal results in more money paid back to your creditors, the Trustee will then file this document and invite your creditors to vote for it during a 45-day period.

Proposals require just a simple majority (i.e. 50% of creditors) to accept it for it to pass and be binding on everyone.

"What's the success rate of getting a Consumer Proposal accepted?"

Consumer Proposals are almost always accepted as they offer a better return to your creditors than if you declared bankruptcy. Creditors will want to help you avoid bankruptcy by accepting your Consumer Proposal, as long as it will result in them recovering a greater amount of what you owe them.

"What does it cost to file a Consumer Proposal?"

Here's the best part — your creditors essentially pay the costs of administration. You make payments to the Trustee, who deducts the costs of administration (mandated by law) before distributing the balance of proceeds to the creditors. There is no extra cost to you above and beyond the monthly payment you have negotiated with your creditors.

"This sounds a lot like Credit Counseling. How is a Consumer Proposal different than what a credit counselor can do for me?"

The main difference is that a Consumer Proposal allows you to pay back just a portion of your total debts (say, 30%) rather than the full amount. A credit counselor can often negotiate a freeze in interest or get some creditors to agree to accept less than the full amount owing, but they have no ability to legally get all of your creditors to abide by the same rules. A Consumer Proposal is a legally binding agreement that is governed by federal law, making it a much more secure and robust tool than what a credit counselor could offer. In addition, income tax debt and student loans can only be included in a consumer proposal.

"OK. But what if I can't afford to pay even a portion of my debts? What does it mean to declare bankruptcy?"

There are so many misconceptions about bankruptcy. Some people say that once you declare bankruptcy you'll never get credit again (which is false). Other people believe that bankruptcy can't be used to release you from income tax debts and student loans (which is also false). Here are some facts:

The decision to declare bankruptcy rests with you and you alone. No one gets "rejected" from bankruptcy. The criteria for declaring yourself bankrupt are that you must owe at least $1,000 and you must be **insolvent.** To be insolvent means that you are unable to pay your bills as they come due.

In order to go bankrupt, your first step is to meet with a federally licensed Trustee in Bankruptcy. Every Trustee in Canada will offer a free initial consultation where you can review your financial options on a confidential, no obligation basis. If you decide that bankruptcy is the right option for you, the Trustee will work with you to prepare the legal documents where you will disclose all of your assets (what you own), all of your debts (what you owe), and your monthly budget (your income and expenses). Once these documents are signed and filed electronically with the federal government, your bankruptcy is now legally binding on all parties involved.

By declaring bankruptcy you are enforcing a "ceasefire" amongst your creditors while you work to restructure your affairs. This means that no creditor is allowed to take any action against you — they are required to deal directly with your Trustee (this means no more collection calls, wage garnishees, or judgment actions against you).

You do not make any further payments on any debts once you declare bankruptcy. However, you will have to pay some fees for the term of your bankruptcy.

"Fees? How much? And for how long will I be in bankruptcy?"

Your bankruptcy payments and the length of time you'll be bankrupt are both driven by the amount of your monthly income. The Trustee will review your income against national low-income cut off levels to determine whether you have any "surplus" income. If you have surplus income, you will be required to make voluntary payments that will be distributed to your creditors as a partial recovery of your debts.

"How much would these payments be per month?"

For 80% of people, bankruptcy lasts for nine months and costs a total of $1,800 (normally payable at $200 per month).

For people who earn above the low-income cut offs (approximately $2,000 monthly cash take home pay for a single person), they will be required to submit monthly budgets for 21 months and will make monthly payments of 50 cents of every dollar above this cut-off level. For example, if you earned $2,500, your payment would be approximately $250 per month. This covers approximately 20% of people who go bankrupt.

For almost everyone that we see, bankruptcy costs far less than what they are already paying each month to service an unmanageable debt load.

"I've heard that I'll lose everything if I go bankrupt. What are the facts?"

The facts are that almost everyone who goes bankrupt keeps all of their assets. Theoretically when you go bankrupt you are abandoning your property for the benefit of your creditors. However, certain provincial laws grant "exemptions" which means that you will not be required to surrender assets that are classified as exempt. These laws vary by province; in BC, for example, you are entitled to keep:

- Household goods, worth up to $4,000 ("garage sale" value, not replacement cost)
- One vehicle, worth up to $5,000
- Equity in a house, worth up to $12,000
- Tools of the Trade, worth up to $10,000
- RRSPs — unlimited, except for contributions in the 12 months prior to bankruptcy
- Essential clothing and medical aids — unlimited

"What's the downside of going bankrupt? What will happen to my credit rating?"

Declaring bankruptcy will have an impact on your credit rating. A first time bankruptcy will be noted on your credit report for six years after your discharge. This does not mean that you'll be unable to get credit again during this time. The granting of credit is a business decision by each creditor and there are certain concrete steps you can take to improve your credit rating in as little as two to three years after your bankruptcy finishes. The most beneficial thing you can do to improve your credit rating is to develop a habit of paying all your bills on time, every month, without exception.

"Who will know about my problems?"

During a Consumer Proposal and nearly all bankruptcies, the only people who will know about your financial problems will be your trustee, the bankruptcy regulator, and your creditors. Theoretically, anyone can pay a fee to search a national bankruptcy database, but it is very rare for this to occur with the per-search fee being a strong deterrent.

...

About the Author: Blair Mantin

Blair Mantin, CMC, CIRP, Trustee in Bankruptcy

Blair Mantin is Vice President of Sands & Associates, BC's largest firm focused exclusively on helping individuals and small businesses solve their financial problems. Blair's career began in corporate strategy consulting with a global professional services firm. International in focus, Blair has resided and served clients in Toronto, Buenos Aires, and London, and now makes Vancouver his home.

Blair is a licensed Trustee in Bankruptcy, a member of the Canadian Association of Insolvency and Restructuring Professionals and a Certified Management Consultant. Blair sits on the Board of the British Columbia Association of Insolvency and Restructuring Professionals (BCAIRP) and was awarded the 2007 Gold Medal for achieving the highest standing amongst new Certified Management Consultants in Canada.

Blair is heavily involved with facilitating access to travel for youth and individuals of limited means. He has served on the National Executive Board of Hostelling International Canada for the past five years as Treasurer, and has been elected Vice President for 2011/2012.

8. When You Need Someone to Talk to at Work

By Karen Seaward

Life Happens

Major life events happen to all of us and can leave us wondering how to cope, how to move forward, or even where to begin.

These events can be positive, such as purchasing your first home or vacation property, winning a large sum of money, making your final mortgage payment, a promotion at work that increases your monthly income, or becoming empty nesters. Or they may be negative events such as separation, divorce, the death of a loved one, parenting responsibilities, or loss of work.

These events — even the happy ones — affect our financial position and can trigger different emotions in each of us. For some, the reaction may be tears or anger, while others may withdraw or depend on drugs or alcohol to numb their feelings. Reactions can become difficult for others to manage, and without a full understanding of why the individual is acting that way, can create distance and damage a relationship.

So what do we do when life happens? What is available to us to begin to process and deal with what is in front of us?

A good starting point is to understand the issue itself and its impact on our life. The key to success is a process of recognizing the problem, creating an action plan, and ensuring the appropriate support is in place. Having a plan with activities and timelines helps us to resolve issues and get back on the right track.

Sounds simple — but in fact it is not. Sometimes the hardest part is understanding what is in our way. For many of us, getting support doesn't come naturally; we try our best to resolve our situation but we don't have the resources or experience. Often we are so caught up in the matter that we are not able to find the correct resource or solution.

Counseling helps users set realistic goals and monitor success, allowing them to resolve issues and create a better balance for themselves.

Many organizations provide employee assistance programs (EAP) that offer services to navigate and resolve issues related to an employee's work, health and life.

EAPs enable employees to take an active role in addressing problems that originate outside of the workplace, and are effective for addressing financial stressors such as debt, creditors or bankruptcy.

Financial issues affect our lives and those in our lives. Each year, people require expert advice about their finances. There are three major areas of focus where life impacts both our finances and our emotions:

1. Credit and debt management
2. Estates
3. Employment status

It's the situations that surround these issues that require focus and attention.

Credit and Debt Problems

When we encounter situations that cause us credit or debt problems, the emotional journey can be tougher then resolving the financial issue itself. This can lead to stress, anxiety, depression, or even drug and alcohol addiction. Take Michelle for example:

Michelle and her husband Jim live in a lovely home in the suburbs with their two children. They would like to enjoy a cottage while also paying down the mortgage on their home, and decide to buy a recreational property for weekend getaways. It's a bit of a stretch with the kids going to university, but it is doable if they watch their finances.

Two years later, Jim loses his job and receives a nine-month severance package with full benefits including extended health. Six weeks after losing his job, Michelle and Jim take a much needed, week-long vacation with their children. The trip provides some relief for Jim in dealing with the anxiety of losing his job.

Upon returning from vacation, Michelle suggests that Jim begin doing repairs on the properties that they haven't gotten around to yet, while also beginning to search for a new job. Jim spends his days undertaking the repair work, networking via lunches and golf games, and distributing his resume.

Eight months later and with many resumes distributed to organizations, Jim is still without work. After thirteen months, Jim still does not have a job and the bills begin to pile up. Michelle doesn't know how to help her husband. Each month as the debt grows, she becomes increasingly distant from her family and friends.

With one call to a counselor Michelle could have begun to plan coping strategies to deal with their debt issues, while receiving help in coping with related emotional issues. In addition, Michelle could have received support from a financial consultation. Dealing with the emotional and financial situation would have resulted in faster resolution and a more fulfilling life for Michelle and her family.

Divorce or Separation

Susan and her husband Frank had been living in a lovely home with their two children. When Susan and Frank decide to separate, Susan and the children choose to remain in the house during the separation. The separation is difficult for her, and she begins to experience many emotions, such as loss and a lack of understanding of where it all went wrong.

Susan has an inside sales job at a pharmaceutical company. Money has never been an issue for Susan and her husband; they've had a mortgage and managed their monthly income appropriately. However, saving money is not easy as their kids are in university and some expected expenses had been incurred over the past few years. When Susan and Frank get to the divorce proceedings, Susan is forced to look at the money situation and realizes she may not be able to afford to live in her home. She needs to find something more affordable, so downsizing is the only option.

Memories from family gatherings, etc. are connected to our homes and moving away from her area and these memories is difficult for Susan. Often she finds herself not just crying over her failed marriage, but also because of the thought of moving away from what she knows. Susan decides to stay in the house, but after the first year her debts exceed her savings so she is forced to move.

Susan begins to focus on her failed marriage. Her feelings of anger cause her to become ineffective at work, withdrawn from family and friends, and upset with her life. Susan goes on disability from her job to cope with the emotional crisis she is experiencing after she is cited for performance issues at work.

Susan needed support a year ago when her divorce was happening, but she relied on her friends (who were angry with her husband). Susan didn't realize that she could access support services at work like an employee assistance program, which could have helped her deal with her divorce and financial concerns before they became a debilitating problem for her, her family and her workplace. Her disability program at work was one that focused on her issues rather than just the medical factors, and helped her gain access to the right support, facilitating a successful return to work and resolution of her issues.

Aging Parents

Baby boomers are growing older and as a result, more of us are in situations where we are helping our aging parents. In my experience, many people feel responsible for their parents' care and safety.

This two-way stretch (of taking care of both elders and children) can lead to stress, preoccupations, time pressures and absence from the workplace. It is becoming difficult to balance the family (parents, partners and children) with work. Parents are living longer and require more support emotionally and in some cases, financially.

For example, Claire has to place one of her parents in a retirement home. Over time, Claire begins to run out of money and the need to either relocate her parent or supplement the financing becomes pressing. The emotional burden of these decisions leads to Claire experiencing feelings of stress, anxiety and depression. Not to mention, she has to take time off from work and must spend increased time away from her family so she can support her parent.

Claire has an employee assistance program that offers financial consultation, elder care consultation and clinical counselor support to ensure she deals with her emotional concerns.

When Life Happens, What Do We See?

Sometimes we are blinded by *how* a situation makes us feel so we can't see *what* actually caused it to happen in the first place. A quality employee assistance program offers the support required to identify and resolve work, health and life issues. Support consists of a counselor who first determines specific causes of the issue and assesses the individual's coping skills and reactions, such as excessive alcohol consumption or overeating. The counselor can then help manage the revealed stress areas through specific changes to the individual's behavior or situation. This may require lifestyle changes to help avoid the situation, or to acknowledge and cope with those things that usually trigger the stress, depression or anxiety. Through counseling, people can uncover things they can do something about, such as rearranging priorities, eliminating imposed obligations, and/or becoming more assertive in areas where you can develop some control over your life. When you feel like you have no control, support from a counselor can help you to deal with your reactions directly and improve your coping skills.

In each case, sound budget planning and identifying and addressing other accompanying issues, such as emotional stressors, are critical components of our journey towards better health. Often, we don't spend our time resolving the right issue. This is because we focus on an event or situational issue, rather than dealing with the cause behind it. In some cases, there may be more than one issue that is creating the situation. As an example, you may deal with a separation or divorce and believe that any financial issues will get sorted out in the process. For instance, someone who is going through a divorce may want to stay in the existing house and may feel more comfortable in either the short or long term staying in the home. It makes going through the divorce easier based on continuity for children, familiarity for you, or simply just not going through so many changes at once. We may seek support for our feelings of divorce, but neglect creating a strategy for a new financial plan to support our new situation. Bills and expenses that were supported by two people are now the responsibility of one. A plan that considers income, support payments or any other income sources is required to ensure a happy, stress-free life.

Short-Term Disability and Impact

Another situation that can impact our financial standing is when we leave work on short-term disability. Those who access disability to deal with a physical or mental health related illness will be impacted financially for a period of time — either by receiving supplemental income or in some cases no income at all. Accessing a line of credit, credit cards or other methods of credit during this time can have negative consequences. Planning for financial impacts of disability is an important step in the recovery process.

Access to financial education programs has proven to be quite effective in helping people make better financial decisions and reduce their financial related stress.

Promoting an employee assistance program in the workplace including proactive financial counseling and consultation services to employees may be particularly helpful in reducing the incidence of more serious financial stressors, which will take a significant toll on both employees and their employers. EAP programs, in particular, are effective for addressing financial stressors (e.g., debt, creditors, bankruptcy, etc.). It is difficult, and in some cases inappropriate, for employers to address financial stressors with their employees directly. EAPs enable employees to take an active role in addressing problems that originate outside of the workplace.

Building the workforce's level of resilience during stressful times is another good strategy. Helping employees to proactively manage and address their stressors can help to mitigate their impact. It is common during highly stressful times for an individual's health and well being to suffer, which significantly and negatively impacts one's ability to cope. Encouraging the adoption of healthy coping behaviors and offering high quality health and wellness programs and services can help to ensure that employees are better able to withstand a stressful time.

Understanding our financial situation and planning for life events is an important factor in ensuring quality of life. Access to support through an EAP can play an important role in effectively managing when life happens, and also strengthen the individual.

...

About the Author: Karen Seaward

Karen Seaward,
Morneau Shepell

Karen Seward is noted for her unique approach of treating health in the workplace as a business issue. She uses quantitative data to illustrate how investment in a healthy workplace drives productivity, offsets disability costs and affects a company's bottom line. Karen is often invited to speak at conferences and seminars, appears in the national media on a regular basis, and has published numerous articles in periodicals including *Benefits Canada* and *Benefits and Pensions Monitor*.

Karen serves as Executive Vice-President responsible for Business Development and Marketing at Morneau Shepell. Here, she leads the enterprise-wide collaboration for growth, generates sales opportunities for the company's largest clients, manages client distribution partner channel relationships and leads the company's marketing and branding initiatives.

Morneau Shepell is Canada's largest human resource consulting and outsourcing firm focused on pensions, benefits, employee assistance programs and workplace health management and productivity solutions. The company offers business solutions that help clients reduce costs, increase employee productivity and improve their competitive positions by supporting their employees' financial security, health and well being.

9. When You're Leaving a Job

By Peter Saulnier

What is Career Transition (Outplacement)?

Career transition, or outplacement as it's often called, is about supporting you when you lose your job. This support can be emotional backing, assistance on how to tell your family about job loss, help to create a results-based resume, strategies to find interesting job opportunities, coaching for an interview, and more.

Career transition services also help you take a strategic approach to your job search, taking into account your needs, personal goals and skills, and matching them with what's going on in the marketplace today.

The organizations that provide these services go by many names: career transition consultants, outplacement providers, career coaches, job search counselors and many more. But they all have one thing in common: they are there to help you move forward in your job search, and in your career.

My New Friend, Anita Jobb

Ann (one of the three Girlfriends who wrote this book) and I have know each other for years, and I know she's a good judge of character, so I was delighted recently when she offered to introduce me to her friend, Anita Jobb. It turns out Anita had just lost her job. After many years with the same company, her position had been "eliminated", as they told her on her last day of work. That day they also told her about career transition services that they were providing for her. She didn't know what that was, so Ann offered to see if I could help. Anita had a number of good questions for me. I answered on behalf of career transition consultants everywhere.

"I'm scared."

Of course you're scared. A job is a pretty important thing for most of us, and it can be nerve-wracking not having one. We can help. First of all, it can be comforting to see that other good people are in the same boat. Frankly, losing a job is something that happens to the best of us, and is actually fairly commonplace today. Moving forward with others, supporting and learning from each other, can be very comforting for most people. Of course, for those who prefer to fly solo, they can go through most career transition services on an individual basis too.

"I already have a resume. What can a career transition consultant do for me?"

That depends what you're looking for. Think of us as a personal coach, or girlfriend, to help you in this transition period. While we can help you create your resume, or help you update and polish the one you've already got, it is only one aspect of the support we provide. We can coach you in a variety of areas. Consider the following:

- What strengths and abilities will you market to a potential employer?
- Are you confident your resume would catch the attention of a recruiting manager out of hundreds that might apply for the same position?
- Do you feel prepared for a behavioral style of interview?
- Are you comfortable building your job search network and expanding it to include information interviews with new contacts?
- Can you confidently negotiate a job offer to your best advantage?

These may seem like daunting questions, but they shouldn't. These are just some of the areas that we can coach you in. A good career consultant will strategize with you to market your strengths and skills to maximize your chances of a successful job search. That's a lot more than simply writing a resume.

"What else do you do?"

Every career transition service is a little different. In addition to the things mentioned above, here are some examples of specific services that might be included in your program:

- In-depth discussions of your future work plans, or entrepreneurial aspirations
- Career, values, and personal interest assessments
- Workshops on the basics of conducting a successful job search

- Regular meetings with a career consultant
- Advice on responding to ads, and using recruiters
- Job searches on the internet, and using social media (such as LinkedIn)
- Interview practice with an experienced interviewer
- Advice on negotiating a pay offer that you'll be thrilled with!
- And more, such as office space, administrative support, and business cards

"Do you find me a job?"

We do better than that: we teach you how to find yourself a job, so that you'll always be equipped with this key life skill, and can face your future feeling confident that you control your own destiny. At least from a career point of view.

"Are you like George Clooney in that movie, *Up In The Air*?"

Good movie. And while I appreciate the comparison to George, the answer is no. In the movie, George Clooney plays Ryan Bingham, who is a type of career transition consultant. For our purposes here, there are two main differences between what he does and the real world of career transition consulting. First, Ryan actually gives employees the news that they are losing their job. This never happens; a manager with the employer company does this. And second, all he does then is give them a folder of information, rather than some actual support and assistance. Enough people have seen the movie that it's become a bit of a mission for me to make sure people know it doesn't reflect reality. Except that all career consultants pretty much look like George, or his female equivalent!

"I've heard that this type of service is going online now. Is that true?"

It's true that the delivery of career transition services online is growing. For example, many providers today have webinars and other services available on their websites. However, most good providers also still have in-person services available. For the majority of individuals, there's nothing like the personal touch to really feel supported in this potentially difficult, but always exciting, journey of career exploration.

"What does career transition consulting have to do with managing money?"

They are connected in a couple of ways. Most obviously, some career transition programs will include assistance from a qualified financial planner, to help you understand your current financial situation, so that you may focus better on your job search or entrepreneurial pursuits. But perhaps more importantly, part of the process is very much what the Girlfriends talk about with respect to values. To illustrate, let me tell you about two different individuals in career transition that I've worked with recently.

The first, Claire, was a professional with a financial services firm. She enjoyed her work, and valued the good salary that it paid her, especially as she was the primary wage earner in a growing family. Claire lost her job when the company laid off a number of employees during a slowdown in their business. She decided to use this event as an opportunity, and worked with her career transition consultant to target more senior positions with other similar companies for her next job. She ended up in a management position with a small but successful firm, at a higher salary than she had been earning in her previous job. Her deliberate career choice led her to a situation where she was earning more income than she had been previously.

The second, Bill, was the executive director of a large trade association. Bill was finding the role very busy, very stressful, and had been struggling in his job for a while. One day Bill was told that he was being terminated, with a good severance package, but no idea what he was going to do next. He had always been successful in his career, moving into increasingly senior roles in fairly rapid succession. But through our self-assessment and career exploration exercises, Bill found that he was beginning to value other elements of life. He decided to look for a less demanding role, and found one as a senior manager with a not-for-profit association. This career choice meant less salary for Bill. But it also meant more quality time with his family, and it was the right choice for him.

"Is there anything else I need to know?"

At the heart of it, career transition support helps people decide what they want to do next in their career and their life, and then helps them get there. Pretty important stuff.

Many people who have taken advantage of these services describe it afterwards as one of the most important experiences they've ever had.

Anita seemed convinced, and called her consultant to book her first appointment.

...

About the Author: Peter Saulnier

Peter Saulnier, Toombs Inc / KWA Partners

Peter Saulnier is Vice President and General Manager with Toombs Inc. / KWA Partners, a leading career management consulting firm, with partner offices across North America and around the world. He has worked in human capital management for over 15 years, with experience in career transition, career management, and employee compensation and benefits.

Peter has been interviewed by and published in various periodicals, including the *Globe and Mail*, *Report on Business* Magazine, *Benefits and Pensions Monitor*, *Canadian HR Reporter*, and the *Vancouver Sun*. He has consulted in Canada, the USA and Asia, and speaks regularly on human capital management issues.

A part-time instructor, Peter is a member of the advisory committee for the business program in HR Management at Kwantlen University College, and is a Director of the Board of the British Columbia Human Resources Management Association. He is the past regional Chair of WorldatWork, the international association of compensation and total reward professionals. Peter holds an MBA with a specialization in Human Resources and Organization Development from the University of British Columbia.

More information on Peter:
linkedin.com/in/petersaulnier

More information on Toombs Inc. / KWA Partners:
www.toombsinc.com
www.kwapartners.com

10. I've Been Fired! What Do I Do Now?

By Greg Heywood

Legal Things to Think about that Affect your Financial Health when Terminated

Well, the unthinkable has happened: you have been fired from your job. Right now you are thinking: how will you tell your family, friends, and colleagues? How will you pay your rent or mortgage? What about that great trip you were saving for?

There is also something else to think about: your legal rights when you are terminated.

The first thing to do is check whether or not you have an employment agreement, as that will tell you whether your employer is obligated to pay you severance (money the employer owes you for the termination) and if so, how much.

If you do not have a copy of your agreement, call your HR (Human Resources) department. They have to send you a copy of your employment agreement. At the same time, if you are unsure you can ask them whether you were fired because you did something wrong, or there was just a shortage of work, or they are restructuring the workplace. (Sometimes in the emotions of the last meeting this gets all mixed up.)

In all jurisdictions, if your employment was terminated for cause (in other words, you engaged in some misconduct such as theft), the employer will be able to terminate your employment and not pay you any severance.

"But I did nothing wrong — I was a great worker and they still fired me. Don't they owe me something?"

If you were terminated and you have an agreement, they owe you the money that the agreement says they would pay you. If you did nothing wrong and you *don't* have an agreement, you might still be eligible for severance.

If you do not have an agreement then the next step will depend upon where you live. In some jurisdictions there are laws that require the employer to pay a minimum severance payment if you are fired without cause. In many jurisdictions in North America, employment is "at will," which means that an employer can let you go for any reason and not pay you anything.

Conversely, in some places, primarily in Canada, there is an obligation to provide notice of termination or severance which can reach as much as two years worth of salary in the most extreme examples. You will need to speak to an attorney to determine what, if any, rights you have.

If you belong to a union, there may be a grievance process available to you so you may have a chance of getting your job back if the termination was not done properly. Also, if you are a member of a union you may have the right to be recalled to your workplace if you were laid off due to lack of work.

"My company wants me to sign a letter accepting the severance. What do I do?"

Generally speaking, if anyone is asking you to sign a document that lasts for a long time, or is about a great deal of money, you should talk to a lawyer. A severance agreement is one of those times. A lawyer can help you negotiate any monies owing to you from your employer. Also, there are several important things you and your lawyer should think about.

Consider whether your health benefits will continue for a period of time or are being terminated immediately. Think about what benefits you need, and have a plan to obtain whatever health care coverage you require. You may have the option of continuing with the group health plans as an individual, although the premium cost will be considerably higher. Generally speaking if you are healthy and can obtain insurance it would be better to obtain new insurance rather than convert the group plan into an individual plan. See the chapter written by Pacific Blue Cross for more information on this topic.

You also may be eligible to apply for income assistance or unemployment insurance. Your eligibility for this assistance will be governed by how long you worked, whether you lost your job as a result of your misconduct, and a few other factors that vary depending upon where you live.

Tax treatment of severance payments varies considerably in each jurisdiction, so seek professional advice on how to shelter your money.

Some options may be to put the money into a retirement plan, to spread the payments over two tax years if you were terminated near the end of the year, or see if the severance can be defined as something other than income (such as compensation for the loss of recall rights, or money for a human rights violation).

If you think that you lost your job because of some form of discrimination, there are additional options for you. In almost all jurisdictions there are laws that prevent an employer from terminating your employment on the basis of your sex, ethnicity, color, age and a number of other characteristics. As the specific laws are different in every area, you will need to consult an attorney to see what, if any, protection you have in your community.

"What are the rules around severance? What do I have to do?"

It is important for you to keep a diary of your efforts to find new employment because after you have been terminated, and if you are seeking severance from your employer, you have a duty to "mitigate" your loss of income. This means that you must honestly look for a new job and that if you fail to do so, it may jeopardize your ability to collect a severance from your employer. If you have a diary of your search efforts you will have the evidence required that you have fulfilled your duty to mitigate.

"Will I have to sue my employer for my money? What will this cost?"

Hopefully not. Most employers are reasonable if you have good information and a good case. However, if you are entitled to a severance payment and you are considering litigation keep in mind that the objective at the end of the day is to have the most money in your pocket after your expenses. You are not fighting your employer just to pay ridiculous lawyer fees. If you need a lawyer they will either charge you by the hour or they will have a contingency agreement where they will keep a certain percentage of your settlement or judgment. Generally speaking contingency fees are in the range of 35% to 45% of your recovery. This is money that you don't get to keep.

The other issue that you need to manage is re-employment. Once you have found a new job, you will have limited your claim for damages, so you will want to settle your dispute as soon as possible if you think you can find another job quickly. Don't be so distracted by spite towards your old employer that you pass up great opportunities for a new position. Focus on the future, not the past. If you are employable, make a quick settlement with your employer even if it is not at top dollar, and then move on with new opportunities.

Losing your job, even if you saw it coming, can be quite unsettling. If it happens, stay focused, don't make it personal, and think about your future. There are other chapters in this book by other people and organizations that can help you through this process. Use them. There is lots of support out there. In a little while, we know your next conversation will be all about your employment letter for your new job!

...

About the Author: Gregory J. Heywood

Greg Heywood,
Roper Greyell LLP

Greg Heywood is married and is the father of three incredible young women; in short he is surrounded by estrogen. He is also a Partner of the firm Roper Greyell LLP. Roper Greyell is a firm that restricts its practice to employment, labor, human rights and immigration law.

Prior to Roper Greyell, Greg was a Partner at a national law firm, and the Director of Labor Relations and in-house counsel with Canadian Airlines International Ltd. Greg was called to the Bars of British Columbia in 1987 and Alberta in 1991.

Greg's focus is on assisting various management clients in all industries by providing strategic advice, and representation before a variety of Boards, Tribunals and the Courts. While Greg is known to be an aggressive litigator, he also works proactively with clients to ensure that the risk of litigation is reduced and opportunities for less adversarial processes are considered. In short, Greg is known for his practical, tactical advice and his skills as an advocate.

11. When You're Looking for a Job

By Molly Huber

Back in the Good Old Days ...

When someone wanted a job 50 years ago, they would furiously scan the "help wanted" ads in the newspaper and circle the ones that were of interest. The next day they would head down to the company to personally hand a resume to the receptionist. This process would be repeated over and over with an occasional phone call to follow up. At the same time, their personal network of friends and relatives were making phone calls, trying to help through one of their contacts. It's also possible that there was a happy father adding a desk alongside his, sure that he would soon be expanding the family business.

"My friends tell me it is all about networking."

They're right. In today's world it is all about networking — and the bigger and more focused it is, the better!

It is important to have a large and targeted network of people that are helping you in your job search. In fact if you do this part right, you are much more likely to quickly find a new position. In today's market, it is important to work within large networking circles in the various industries or professional groups. By targeting groups, you can invest more time in building the relationships that will improve your chances of being considered for the role you want. Take the time early in your job search to identify what industries, companies and positions are of the greatest interest to you. Write it down. This list becomes the foundation of building your networks and targeting your job search in the most effective manner.

"How can a recruitment company help me?"

A recruitment company is in business to help people find exciting and challenging new job opportunities, and to simultaneously help client companies secure great new staff. Recruiters have great connections and can use them to help you. Having a staffing agency as part of your professional network is an absolute must.

I can tell you that if you find yourself in any of the following situations it's a great idea to start to build a relationship with a Recruiter in your particular industry or trade.

"I've lost my job."

Sometimes losing your job can be the best thing to happen to your professional career. It can give you an opportunity to re-examine your different passions, and find a new position to satisfy your current professional "wants."

A good Recruiter is someone who can give you perspective on the conditions of the current market and point you in the direction of industries that are in growth mode, rather than those in decline. They can give you guidance on appropriate salaries and trends in the overall employment market, as well as within your professional peer group. They can advise you on the viability of changing your profession, and help you figure out what that next great career step might look like.

"I need a short term job."

And then there are the times when losing your job is the worst thing that could ever happen, and you don't exactly have the financial support to luxuriously re-examine your professional path!

Heck, you may not have the ability to make rent based on the limited severance that you may (or may not!) have received. In times like these you need people immediately getting you into a new job! Many staffing agencies place candidates into both temporary and long-term positions, and if time is of the essence it's a great reason to seek the help of a staffing agency. The network you need to build, and develop relationships with, has already been well established by the recruitment and staffing firm, reducing a large amount of up front time.

In addition to helping you to continue to look for your dream job, they are also often able to find a short-term assignment that would help ensure that you're able to take care of your every day life. Who knows, maybe one of those temporary assignments ends up being your dream job! Staffing agencies can help you to transition through temporary and into permanent employment, and can also help you to find immediate employment to help you to pay the bills.

"My company is in trouble and I may need a job in the future."

There are very few of us who have the same sense of job security as our parents did. In today's job market, you may find yourself in a place where, regardless of how well you're performing in your job, there's the possibility of a lay-off based on circumstances beyond your control. This uncertainty can cause you anxiety that will manifest itself both mentally and physically! A relationship with a Recruiter can act as a contingency plan just in case. Knowing a Recruiter can give you the same sense of safety as you feel in knowing that you've got a spare tire in the trunk, just in case you ever run over a nail.

"I want to be a consultant — but getting new clients is tough!"

Becoming an expert in your field has its advantages, and one of those advantages is that others may be very interested in gleaning both skill and information from you. When you're considering moving into a consulting role, a Recruiter can help lead the way. By their very nature, consulting positions are temporary, and therefore you have to become an expert in not only your field, but also finding new consulting opportunities. In addition to helping you find the positions, Recruiters can also give you some advice on the logistics of the consulting industry.

"OK, so I understand that I need to build a relationship with a Recruiter, but how do I do that?"

Finding the right Recruiter is like starting any new relationship; it's important to find the right match for your personality, and to take things one step at a time! Also similarly to a new boyfriend, it's important to find someone who listens to you and cares about what you say, feel, and want.

Strong ethics are important in any good relationship, and a positive outlook never hurt! The only difference with a Recruiter is that you also want them to have a strong understanding of how best to help you secure a new position. Ask a number of prepared questions to ensure that they indeed understand the market conditions, the industries and careers you would like to target, and most importantly, that they have a clearly defined set of professional values.

In addition to finding the right fit with your Recruiter, it's also important to consider the company that they work for. It's important to work with reputable staffing agencies, with strong business ties to the industry that you are pursuing so that they can open lots of doors and facilitate many new introductions.

A good starting point for this is asking within your own network. I'm confident you'll find someone who can facilitate an introduction on your behalf. Failing that, look online to see who the staffing industry experts are, and start with those companies. Give them a call. Prepare a short introduction like the following — and I am sure that they will help you!

Introduction:

"Hi, I am X. I noticed that you are advertising for Y positions. I have experience in this area and was hoping that we could spend a couple of minutes getting to know each other to see if it makes sense for us to talk further about the specifics of my background, and the typical needs of your clients."

See, wasn't that easy?

"How do I prepare for my first meeting with the Recruiter?"

It's important to prepare for a meeting with a Recruiter in the same way that you would for any other interview. Make sure you bring your resume and are prepared to talk about your skills and experiences. Make sure that you dress as if you were going to an interview. Take a look at the website of the company and familiarize yourself with the positions that they currently have available. Overall, it is important to make a good first impression as the recruiter will be trying to picture where you can best fit amongst their clients.

"How do I determine if the recruitment agency and Recruiters will be a good fit for me?"

Most first meetings are done at the Recruiter's location. Look around you. Does it look like a professional office? Does the Recruiter greet you professionally? Does the Recruiter talk sensibly about the industry? Trust your gut instincts. If the Recruiter and the agency do not appear professional — leave. There are good agencies out there that will properly represent you and your skills.

"How much will it cost me?"

The easiest question of them all! Nothing. In fact, in Canada it's illegal to charge candidates for the service provided by staffing agencies such as the one I work for.

...

About the Author: Molly Huber

Molly Huber, Randstad Technologies

Molly Huber has been a "Girlfriend" to thousands of employees over the last 10 years. She has helped them reach their financial and career goals in challenging and interesting employment opportunities, while simultaneously helping companies to grow by engaging productive talent. Her strong foundation in the recruitment industry enables her to be a valuable asset to IT professionals and the companies that hire them.

Molly is currently Vice President of the Western Region of Randstad Technologies, overseeing operations west of Ontario including branches in Vancouver, Calgary, Edmonton, Winnipeg, Victoria and Regina.

Randstad Technologies is a member of the Randstad Canada group of companies. They are the largest provider of staffing, recruitment and HR Services in Canada. As the only fully integrated staffing company in the country, they provide a unique, full range of capabilities, from professional staffing in various industries such as engineering and IT, HR end-to-end programs such as recruitment and payroll process outsourcing, to vendor management solutions — no other staffing company in the country offers such a wide variety of services.

Randstad Canada provides unrivalled expertise in matching job seekers with select employers throughout their 60+ branches. Randstad Canada is part of Randstad Holding nv, the world's second largest recruitment and HR services provider. Randstad has expanded to serve more than 40 countries across North America, South America, Europe, Asia, Africa and Australia, representing over 90% of the global HR services market, and holds a top three position in many of the world's key markets. Since its foundation, Randstad has worked constantly on expanding its vision, capabilities and service offerings.

12. Just Got that Dream Job!

By Greg Heywood

You are so excited; you've just been offered a job at a great company. You can't wait to start! But they are asking you to sign a long employment letter. What is this all about? What do you need to know before you sign it?

An employment agreement will define your roles and responsibilities, your salary and benefits, the amount of vacation you are entitled to take, and a host of other issues that are key to your job. While nobody wants to think about an ending when they are just beginning, an employment agreement will define your severance entitlement in the event your employment is terminated.

You can negotiate any of these points. However, some employers are less likely to move on these points than others. Make sure you can live with these rules as they bind you for the length of the agreement.

Don't forget to always keep a copy of this agreement with your financial documents.

"What are the most common things to find in an employment agreement?"

I have compiled a list explaining the common parts of an employment agreement. If you have questions it's a good idea to see a lawyer — remember this agreement will bind you to the employer for a long time. As a general rule any document you sign that lasts for a long period of time, or is about a large sum of money, should be reviewed by a lawyer. An employment agreement is both — long lasting and about a lot of money.

This is a checklist of things that should be in your employment agreement — and that you have the right to negotiate when you start a new job. Descriptions and definitions are below the list.

- Nature of agreement — full time, part time, consultant or contractor?
- Term of agreement — how long this will last
- Non-Solicit and Non-Compete agreement
- Compensation including benefits
- Dispute Resolution
- Termination

Nature of the relationship: While many of us are employees, a growing number of people are independent contractors. If you are a contractor as opposed to an employee, the company that hires you usually doesn't deduct payroll tax, provide any health benefits, or expect you to maintain the same regular hours as an employee. The benefit for you is that your hourly rate may be higher and you may be able to write off some of your income. (Tax laws vary by location; see your tax expert or accountant for details).

Term of the agreement: Many agreements are indefinite, which means that they will run until one of the parties terminates the agreement. Some employment agreements are for a fixed period of time, or are project based.

Non-Solicit and Non-Compete agreements: Depending on the nature of your position, your employer may include these obligations in your employment agreement, or want you to sign a separate agreement. If you can get away without including these obligations, do so.

Typically **Non-Solicit agreements** prevent you from taking customers and employees away from your former employer for a period of time after your termination. These agreements can continue for anywhere from six months to two years following your departure from the company.

A **Non-Compete** agreement is more restrictive in that it is intended to prevent you from working in the industry. Often these restrictions are limited by time and distance from the employer's place of business. In some jurisdictions, such as California, non-compete agreements are not enforceable. A non-compete agreement can significantly impact your ability to apply your knowledge and skills following your departure from your employer.

Compensation: Of course you want your salary defined, but there are also other issues such as stock options, bonuses, pension contributions, benefit plans, vacation, automobile allowance and club memberships. If there is a bonus plan, is it discretionary (in other words completely up to the company) or is it performance based? If it is the latter, at least you will have some control over whether you earn a bonus if the targets that they set are reasonable. Find out what their targets are.

Dispute Resolution: Many employment agreements have arbitration clauses so that in the event of a dispute the matter does not end up in court. This may or may not be a good thing for you, depending upon the cost of dealing with your dispute in court or in arbitration. Generally speaking you want the fastest and the cheapest dispute resolution process.

Termination: Any good employment agreement will provide some guidance on the parties' obligations upon termination. You will want to define what your severance will be in the event your employment is terminated without cause. Severance agreements can be structured in a number of ways: upon termination you might receive a lump sum of money, or you may be entitled to salary continuance where you are not required to work, but your employer will continue to pay you for a period of time. Generally speaking you will want to bargain for the lump sum severance.

When you begin a new employment relationship, assess the balance of power. Are you lucky to get the job or do they really need you? The more they need you the firmer you can be with your demands. This may be the time to ask for that extra week of vacation, as it is usually very difficult to change those things once you are inside the door.

Other benefits that you may wish to negotiate include payment of professional fees, and commitment and funding for professional training and development. If you are joining an employer with offices scattered about the country, do you want the ability to move or do you want to stay within your city? The more issues you can resolve up front the fewer surprises you will discover down the road.

...

About the Author: Gregory J. Heywood

Greg Heywood,
Roper Greyell LLP

Greg Heywood is married and is the father of three incredible young women; in short he is surrounded by estrogen. He is also a Partner of the firm Roper Greyell LLP. Roper Greyell is a firm that restricts its practice to employment, labor, human rights and immigration law.

Prior to Roper Greyell, Greg was a Partner at a national law firm, and the Director of Labor Relations and in-house counsel with Canadian Airlines International Ltd. Greg was called to the Bars of British Columbia in 1987 and Alberta in 1991.

Greg's focus is on assisting various management clients in all industries by providing strategic advice, and representation before a variety of Boards, Tribunals and the Courts. While Greg is known to be an aggressive litigator, he also works proactively with clients to ensure that the risk of litigation is reduced and opportunities for less adversarial processes are considered. In short, Greg is known for his practical, tactical advice and his skills as an advocate.

Conclusion

So Long, Farewell …

We're at the end of the book. But never at the end of our financial journeys. We three Girlfriends learned a lot while writing this book (mostly about patience!) and we continue to learn every day. We hope our stories, lessons and exercises helped you to discover your personal values and develop financial goals and action plans to support those values that are uniquely yours.

We hope that you are building a support network of family and friends, as well as experts who can help you through times of need and uncertainty.

We hope you agree with the importance of giving back to your community with charity and as a role model of financial health.

Most of all, we hope that you appreciate your unique values and continue to spend and save in accordance with your own financial goals and action plans.

But Wait, There's More …

We had such a great time making this book that we've continued the conversation. Follow us on Twitter at @moneygirlfriend or on our Facebook page *Girlfriends Guide to Money*, and come visit us at GirlfriendsGuidetoMoney.com. We have great conversations, articles, worksheets and creative activities. You can learn more about us and introduce yourself. We'd love to hear your story!

Endnotes

Thanks, Friends

We are so grateful for the love and support of those who helped make this book a reality. We especially want to thank Greg Heywood of Roper Greyell LLP; Molly Huber of Randstad Technologies; Peter Saulnier of Toombs Inc. / KWA Partners; Paul Stephens of Pacific Blue Cross; Blair Mantin of Sands & Associates; Karen Seaward of Morneau Sheppell; the Teldon Media Group; Joe Goodwill; and Adrian Van Viersen for their expertise and support of our objectives.

We'd like to thank our families for their feedback, support and input. Thanks to all our readers and reviewers for their time, energy and excellent insight. And thanks to you for being willing to improve the world by improving your life.

Girlfriends Give Back

We Girlfriends have a few favorite charities, one of which is Covenant House Vancouver. We are donating 20% of the profits from this book to them. For more information on our other charitable activities, please check the "Girlfriends Give Back" section on our website at girlfriendsguidetomoney.com.

Covenant House Vancouver

 Covenant House Vancouver is honored to be the one of the charities of choice for a portion of the proceeds from the sale of this book. We would like to thank Ann, Lucinda and Marina for thinking of our young people in need while providing such valuable information to girlfriends around the world.

Covenant House is an international organization assisting over 55,000 homeless young people each year in Canada, United States and Central America.

Every day we provide food, housing and support to help these young people heal from the traumas of their past and to learn the skills that they will need to live independent lives, free from the street.

To learn more about Covenant House Vancouver please go to covenanthousebc.org. Thank you for helping us to find an answer to homelessness, one young person at a time.

Information on Covenant House International is available at Covenanthouse.org.

About the Authors

Ann Leckie

Ann Leckie

Ann is a nationally recognized author and keynote speaker. An expert in Human Resources, Ann has appeared on local and national media including *CBC The National*, and is a keynote speaker at industry conferences. She is the author of two award-winning textbooks on disability management currently used in Canadian post secondary business courses.

Ann has been an innovative and integral team member with a variety of large companies in the insurance, financial, retail, media, and personal services sectors.

Ann received her Honors degree in Arts from Queens University, and continued her education at the British Columbia Institute of Technology, earning a Post Graduate Diploma in Human Resources, and later the Certified Employee Benefits Specialist Designation.

Ann lives in Vancouver BC with her family. She practices Taekwondo, and recently achieved her Black Belt designation.

Lucinda Atwood

Lucinda Atwood

Lucinda is a writer and editor. She is a graduate of Dundas Valley School of Art, Sheridan Institute of Technology, and The Western Front (Media Design).

Currently both a teacher and a student at Emily Carr University, Lucinda brings creativity and curiosity to her projects and processes. A skilled teacher and inspired communicator, she says "my favorite compliment is being told that I changed the way someone sees the world."

Lucinda lives in Vancouver BC where she practices artmaking, Chi Running and yoga. She writes about life and happiness at lucindaatwood.com.

Marina Glass

Marina Glass

Marina is an entrepreneur, community leader and life skills coach. For the past 15 years she has run a business strategy consultancy servicing Fortune 500, municipal and provincial government clients. Marina's success is built on a unique combination of creative solutions, strategic understanding, conflict resolution and mediation skills. Her background in project management ensures that vision and ideation is embodied in a realistic project delivery approach.

Marina studied at Simon Fraser University, the British Columbia Institute of Technology and the Justice Institute of BC. Marina is passionately dedicated to equal opportunities and is a member of the Learning Disabilities Association. She helped transform the Exceleration Triathlon and Multisport club from a fledgling sports club into a hugely successful non-profit organization dedicated to bringing sports participation to families of all economic and cultural backgrounds.

Marina is directing her many years of experience and leadership with not-for-profit and children in-need organizations toward coaching adults. Her knowledge and perseverance in identifying issues, finding and connecting people with resources and removing barriers to success make Marina an invaluable leader for individuals and business alike.

She has traveled the world extensively, including living in Croatia, France, England, Holland and throughout Canada. Marina calls Vancouver BC home, along with her husband of 14 years, two kids and a menagerie of pets.